COLOUR *to the* WILDFLOWERS *of Central and Western Australia*

DENISE GREIG

Angus&Robertson
An imprint of HarperCollins*Publishers*

AN ANGUS & ROBERTSON BOOK
An imprint of HarperCollinsPublishers

First published in Australia in 1992 by
CollinsAngus&Robertson Publishers Pty Limited (ACN 009 913 517)
A division of HarperCollinsPublishers (Australia) Pty Limited
25-31 Ryde Road, Pymble NSW 2073, Australia

HarperCollinsPublishers (New Zealand) Limited
31 View Road, Glenfield, Auckland 10, New Zealand

HarperCollinsPublishers Limited
77-85 Fulham Palace Road, London W6 8JB, United Kingdom

National Library of Australia
Cataloguing-in-Publication data:

Greig Denise, 1945 –
Colour guide to the wildflowers of Central and Western Australia.

Includes index.
ISBN 0 207 17065 7.

1. Wild flowers —Australia, Central —Identification. 2. Wild flowers —Western Australia —Identification. I. Title.

582.130994

Printed in Hong Kong

5 4 3 2 1
96 95 94 93 92

In memory
of my friend
Matthew Robinson

Contents

Introduction

^ ^ ^

Colour Guide to Wildflowers of Central and Western Australia is a companion volume to *Colour Guide to Wildflowers of Eastern Australia*. Both books were written for people who are unfamiliar with Australian plants and need help in identifying common wildflowers.

This easy to use guide will help you identify the beautiful flowers of Central and Western Australia. It has been divided into six colour groups, so that when you discover a flower, simply open the book at the appropriate colour section and scan the photographs for a flower that looks similar. Around three hundred species are photographed and described — they represent some of the most common and familiar plants you are likely to encounter growing in the wild. In many cases, the photograph will lead you to the exact species, although sometimes where there is a large number of species involved you may only be able to track your flower to a genus. As there are many thousands of flowering plants in Central and Western Australia, there are of course many that are not mentioned. However, once you have discovered the delights of identifying the more common wildflowers, you may be stimulated to seek out some of the rarer plants.

This guide is not designed to sit on the bookcase. It is to be carried with you when you go for a walk or picnic. The book is small enough to take up permanent residence in the camera bag, picnic basket, backpack or glove box of the car, so that you have it handy.

Many people want to know more about our beautiful wildflowers and being able to identify them helps us to appreciate the Australian bush. This natural environment has an exciting and varied flora and, fortunately much of the bushland is accessible. This book should help you enjoy it to the fullest.

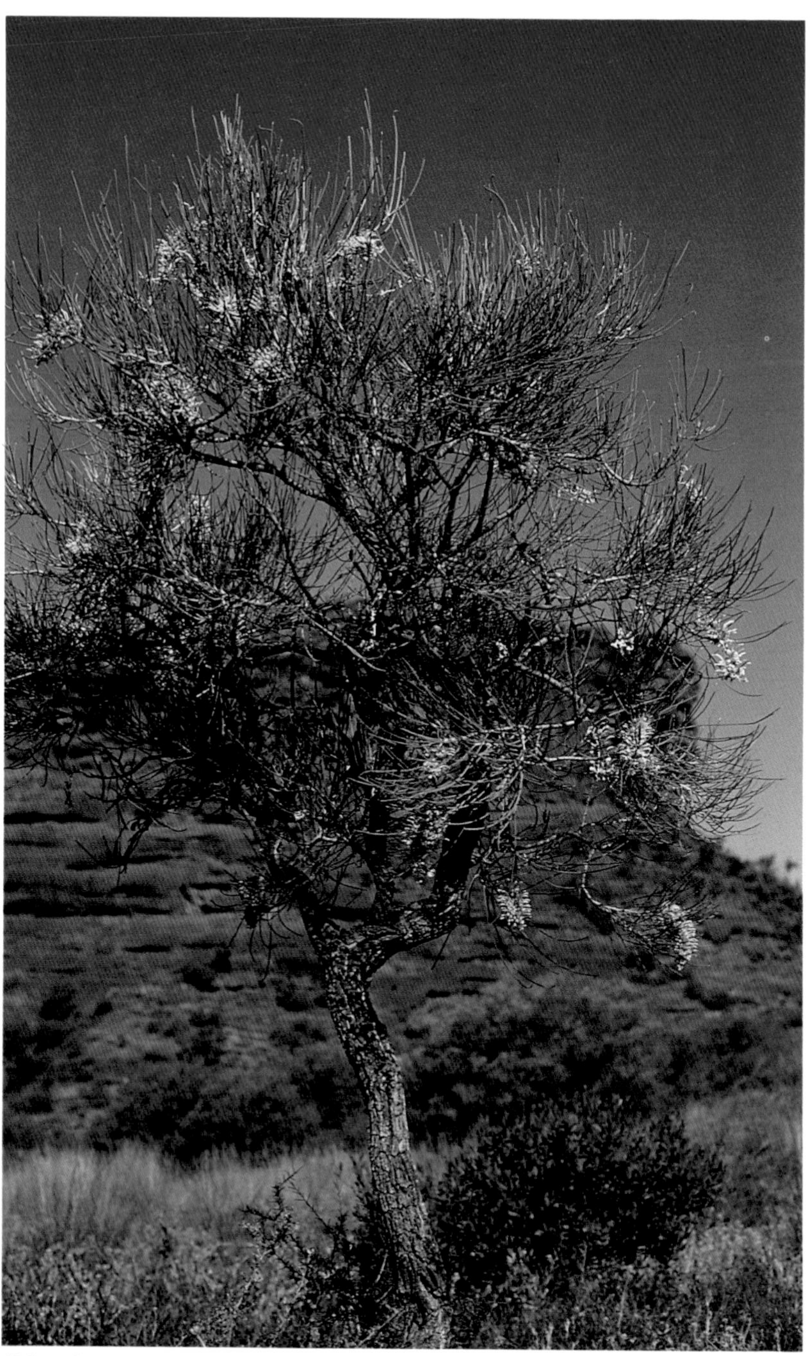

Hakea suberea.

Finke Gorge, Northern Territory.

Glossary

^ ^ ^

Acute: ending in a sharp point.
Alternate: arranged at different levels along a stem, not opposite.
Annual: a plant which completes its life cycle in one year.
Anther: the top of the stamen which contains the pollen.
Apex: the tip of an organ, such as a leaf or petal.
Aromatic: fragrant.
Axil: the angle between a stem and leaf.
Axillary: borne in an axil.
Biennial: a plant that completes its life cycle in two years.
Bipinnate: having pinnate leaves in which the leaflets are again divided into secondary leaflets.
Bract: a leaf-like structure which surrounds or encloses a flower or group of small individual flowers.
Calyx: the outer series of floral leaves, each one a sepal.
Canopy: the cover of foliage of a tree or community.
Capsule: a dry fruit that opens when mature to release the seeds.
Carnivorous: flesh-eating; applied to those plants which digest insects.
Corolla: the whole of the petals of a single flower.
Cultivar: a variety of a plant produced in cultivation.
Cylindrical: cylinder-like in shape with both sides more or less parallel.
Deciduous: falling or shedding of any plant part at the end of the growth period.
Dentate: toothed on the margin.
Dormant: temporary inactive growth.
Drupe: a succulent fruit with a stone enclosing the seed or seeds.
Endemic: confined to a particular region or location.
Entire: of leaf, without toothing or division.
Epiphyte: a plant which grows on another plant, but not as a parasite.
Erect: upright.
Exotic: a plant introduced from a foreign country.
Family: a group of genera botanically related.
Follicle: a dry fruit containing more than one seed which splits open along one side only; for example, the fruit of hakeas and grevilleas.
Frond: the leaf of a fern or palm.

Genus: a natural group of closely related species (plural is genera).

Glabrous: smooth, without hairs.

Gland: a liquid-secreting organ, usually on leaves.

Glaucous: covered with bloom, giving a greyish or powdery appearance.

Globular: rounded or ball-shaped.

Habitat: the environment in which a plant grows.

Head: a compact cluster of flowers.

Herbaceous: plant without woody stems.

Hirsute: covered with long coarse hairs.

Hoary: densely covered with short, whitish pubescence.

Inflorescence: the flower structure of a plant.

Indigenous: original to the country—not introduced.

Insectivorous: feeding on insects. Plants which capture insects and absorb nutriment from them.

Labellum: front petal of an orchid appearing as a lip or tongue.

Lanceolate: shaped like the head of a lance, broadest in the lowest half and tapering to both ends.

Lateral: occurring at the side.

Liane: a large woody climber.

Lichen: a plant organism composed of fungus and algae forming a crust on rocks, tree trunks and soil.

Linear: long and narrow with more or less parallel sides.

Lobe: a rounded division of leaf, petal or other plant organ.

Longitudinal: in the direction of the length.

Margin: the edge of a leaf.

Mid-rib: the main central vein that runs the full length of a leaf.

Monoecious: male and female flowers on the same plant.

Oblanceolate: lance-shaped leaf, broader toward the tip.

Orbicular: circular or almost.

Ovate: egg-shaped with the broadest part at the base.

Panicle: an irregular, much-branched spray of flowers.

Peduncle: stalk of a flower cluster or individual flower.

Pendulous: hanging downwards.

Perennial: a plant with a life span of more than two years.

Phyllode: a flattened leaf stalk which functions as a leaf.

Pinnate: a compound leaf, divided once with leaflets arranged on each side of central stalk.

Prostrate: lying closely on the gound.
Pseudobulb: bulb-like thickened stem of some orchids.
Pubescent: covered with short, soft hair; downy.
Pungent: terminating in a stiff, sharp point.
Raceme: an unbranched spray of equally stalked flowers along a common stem.
Recurved: curved backward or downward.
Resinous: covered with sticky substance.
Rhizome: a creeping underground stem.
Rosette: an arrangement of leaves radiating from a centre, usually near the ground.
Saprophyte: a plant which lives on dead organic matter.
Sessile: without a stalk.
Solitary: borne singly or alone.
Spathe: a large leafy bract enclosing a flower cluster.
Spike: an arrangement of stalkless flowers along an individual stem.
Stamen: the male portion of a flower, which comprises a pollen-bearing anther and supporting filament.
Stellate: star-shaped.
Stigma: the part of the flower that receives the pollen.
Tendril: a twisting thread-like shoot of a leaf or stem by which a climbing plant may hold itself in position.
Terete: slender and circular in cross-section.
Terminal: at the end or apex.
Terrestrial: growing in the ground.
Trifoliate: a compound leaf having three leaflets.
Tuber: the swollen end of an underground stem or stolon.
Umbel: a cluster of individual flower stalks all arising from the same point.
Undulate: wavy.
Valve: the segment of a capsule which splits to release the seeds.
Whorl: a ring of flower petals or leaves encircling a stem.

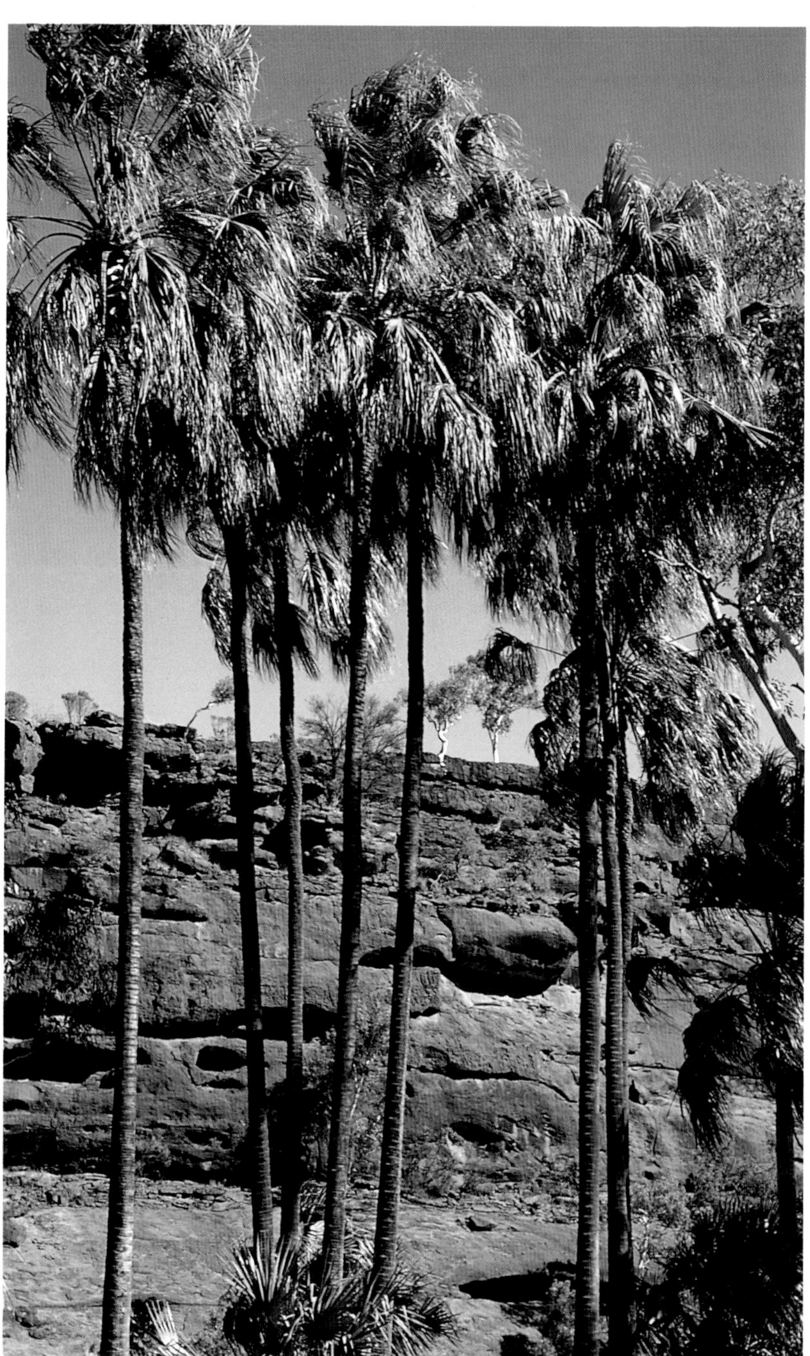

Livistona mariae.
Palm Valley, Northern Territory.

How to Use This Book

^ ^ ^

The plant species in this book are grouped according to the colour of their flowers. The six colour groups are as follows:

1. White and Cream
2. Yellow
3. Pink
4. Orange and Red
5. Purple and Blue
6. Green and Unusual Colours

In each section, the genera are arranged in alphabetical order and within each genus the species are also listed alphabetically. The name of the family to which each species belongs is listed after the name of the species. Although many Australian plants do not have common names, if a common name is in general usage it is included beneath the botanical name.

Under the family name, the State or in some cases the States where the plant naturally occurs is listed. A number of species mentioned are widespread and can be found in all States. Standard abbreviations are used for the names of States.

The Plants Described

The species described and illustrated are those most likely to be seen in often frequented places in Central and Western Australia.

The text deals only with flowering plants and includes orchids, annuals, herbaceous plants and shrubs. Only a few trees are listed and these are the colourful, large-flowered mallees seen mostly in the South-west Province of Western Australia.

Ferns, fungi, sedges, grasses and plants introduced from other countries are not included.

The descriptions of the plants are in non-technical terms and emphasise prominent characteristics such as plant size, foliage arrangement and shape, and floral structure, as well as any other obvious features which may assist in identification.

Plant sizes vary greatly in different environments and climates. The size mentioned is that of the common form of the species. Most plants have both large and some very small leaves. Leaf measurements refer to the average mature size of the leaf.

When comparing a flower with a photograph, carefully check the description of the plant to be sure you have the right species. In some cases you might find that your flower and the photograph are very similar, but do not exactly fit the description. Within the confines of this small book we cannot include all the species you might find growing in the wild, but at least you might discover to which genus the flower belongs and this information will assist you in further study of these plants.

Identification by colour photographs has its limitations and often photographs do not reproduce a true colour of the flower. There are also often colour variations within a species and indefinable hues such as pinky-mauve and purplish-red. It is a good idea to check more than one section of the book if colour variation is suspected. While botanical terminology has been kept to an absolute minimum a glossary has been included to assist the reader in understanding some of the terms.

Growing Wildflowers

Throughout the book mention is made of those species which are successful in cultivation and which are readily available from nurseries which sell native plants. A good native plant nursery will give you advice and some information about what species of plants will grow well under your garden's conditions.

Plants which have been propagated and hardened under nursery conditions are those most likely to flourish in your garden. Within our National Parks and wilderness areas all plants, including the wildflowers they produce, are protected by law and should not be removed. The wildflowers which we so admire should be left to give similar pleasure to those bushwalkers who follow.

Eucalyptus torquata.
Coolgardie, Western Australia.

Photographing Wildflowers

^ ^ ^

Photographing plants and flowers in the countryside is creative and challenging and is a good healthy excuse to visit and browse in the bush. It is also a great aid in the identification and recording of species in their natural habitats. The bushland offers wonderful subjects in any season, and plant photography does not have to rest with a showy flower. Lichens, mosses, grasses and fungi all make striking subjects. Patience, care, a little thought and some good equipment will go a long way towards giving you a pleasing photograph.

Equipment

Most plant photography is satisfactorily performed with a 35 mm single-lens reflex camera. While stunning artistic shots can be taken with black and white film, most plant photographers prefer to use colour slide film. Colour negative film usually produces poor quality prints.

A 55 mm macro lens will enable you to take close-up detailed shots. Most macro lenses have a built-in maximum magnification of 1/2, but you can get higher magnification by adding extension rings or a bellows unit to your system.

An electronic flash will allow you to control conditions such as poor light, distracting backgrounds and wind movement. A UV filter will cut down on ultraviolet light, thus reducing the bluish cast in colour films. It will also protect your lens from dust and rain and constant wiping.

One accessory essential to good plant photography is a sturdy tripod. This will permit critical focusing, especially in close-up work, and reduce the possibility of blurred photographs through camera movement. Often it is impractical to use a tripod if locations are rough or if you need to lie flat on your stomach to take the photograph. Bear in mind that using a hand-held camera with the shutter speed set slower than 1/60 second will not result in a sharp picture and you will need some sort of improvised support. A small pillow stuffed with rice or small dried beans is light to carry and can be easily moulded to cushion your camera to prevent camera movement.

Background

One of the main problems of photographing a flower in the field is dealing with a confusing or busy background. It has often been suggested an artificial background of a coloured card be used to block out the background, but how is it possible to achieve a good natural flower photograph with a flat, coloured background? Often the problem of a bush background can very easily be solved by changing your viewpoint by kneeling, squatting, bending, stooping or lying flat on your stomach. Rarely do you find a good specimen in the right position that you can photograph while standing up straight; you must be prepared to move around — unknown to most people, plant photography keeps you very fit. A low viewpoint using the sky as a background can often be very effective, or try lining up the shot in front of a large tree trunk to eliminate background clutter. Consider using other flowers on the bush or choose a different plant of the same species.

When taking close-ups of individual flowers, the subject often fills the frame and considerations of background can be forgotten. Also, depth of focus is very small and background elements are often blurred while the subject is in sharp focus.

An electronic flash can be used to highlight the subject and darken the distracting shapes in the background by contrast, but this can add an element of artificiality and in some cases a black background to the shot.

Weather Conditions

Ideally the best weather conditions for flower photography are a warm, still day with a slightly overcast sky. Direct light from a full sun in the middle of the day tends to bleach out detail, especially in pastel-coloured or white flowers. Also a full sun, particularly in the afternoon, casts strong shadows on the subject and this may seriously affect the result. If you have some assistance you can create diffused light from direct sunlight by using a sheet of tracing paper held between the flower and the sun. Diffused lighting also helps to maintain a truer colour in blue and purple flowers, which may take on a pinkish cast when photographed in full sun.

On heavy overcast days a flash can be used to supplement light. A flash is also needed when photographing in rainforests, where the available light is usually totally inadequate.

Windy weather is the curse of all flower photographers. Quite often, however, you might need only to wait for the flowers to pause in the breeze. Other times it may seem that the wind will never stop and a fast shutter speed of 1/125 second or more might be needed to eliminate blur due to flower motion caused by the wind. A flash can also be used to eliminate movement.

With plant photography a new and fascinating world awaits you. Putting names to the photographed flowers becomes almost an addiction and is one of the most exciting and fastest ways imaginable of improving your knowledge and love of the Australian countryside.

Where to Find Wildflowers

^^^

Plants have no sense of state borders and those included here from Central Australia take in the areas most travelled around Alice Springs, Uluru (Ayers Rock), inland South Australia and the Nullarbor Plain.

Most of the plants described for Western Australia are from the botanical zone known as the South-west Province which takes in an area roughly from Shark Bay, north of Perth, to Israelite Bay, east of Esperance. Some plants which occur in the botanical regions known as the South-western Interzone and Eremaean Province are also included as they can be easily seen along well-used roads and sometimes overlap with plants of Central Australia.

Central Australia

Many visitors to Central Australia expect to see vast inhospitable desert areas devoid of plant life. This may be true if you travel in mid summer after a prolonged dry spell. However, most people choose to journey through Australia's heart during the cooler months of winter and early spring. In the dry season it is possible to travel on many inland roads in a conventional car. This is the most pleasant time to travel inland and after good rain you may even be lucky enough to see the wonderful—but brief—blanketing 'Persian' carpet effect of wildflowers in profusion.

Whether the rainfall has been good or not a rich variety of plants actually manage to live, grow and flower well—from the low-lying parakeelyas and rugged wattles to tall eucalypts and desert oaks. In protected locations among the vividly-coloured rocks of Standley Chasm in the Macdonnell Ranges, Northern Territory, there are even a few soft little ferns and the magnificent ancient cycad, *Macrozamia macdonnellii,* reminding us of the inland seas which receded millions of years ago.

Many plants of the inland have developed characteristics to enable them to avoid excessive loss of moisture during the high summer temperatures and yet withstand severe desert frosts. Adaptations for survival include succulent, water-storing leaves; greyish-bluish foliage; thick, fleshy roots; protective, thick, corky bark; or controlled dormancy in seeds, which allows germination only after soaking rains. During prolonged dry spells many desert plants shed their leaves: these are usually small and often covered with a tough waxy coating to reduce loss of moisture. Leaves are sometimes absent entirely, reduced to tiny scales such as in the desert oak, *Allocasuarina decaisneana*, or replaced with sharp spines like those found on the vicious dead finish, *Acacia tetragonophylla*.

The most dominant plant of Central Australia is the hardy mulga, *Acacia aneura*, whose narrow, silvery leaves are designed to reflect the intense sunlight and reduce heat absorption. It also spreads its roots out just below the surface to exploit the moisture from showers and thunderstorms. Where a group of mulgas have formed a thicket you may find silver lichen growing on the trunks. This growth occurs only on the southern side of the trunks, so if you get lost you can instantly line up direction.

When travelling in Central Australia many kilometres will be through country covered in spinifex. There are several types of spinifex, *Trioda* species, all of which are incredibly prickly. Spinifex grows by repeatedly growing outwards. As one of the outer branches bends downwards it takes root and forms a new plant. This is why you may see large clumps forming rings or crescent shapes as they begin to die out in the centre. If the plant life becomes really monotonous you could play 'spot the perfect spinifex ring'.

The *Eremophila* genus has a wealth of colourful spring flowers. The name is derived from the Greek work *eremos* (a desert), and *philo* (to love), referring to the semi-arid and arid habitats of many of the species. They are able to withstand severe drought and often display leaf adaptations such as a coating of a varnish-like substance or fine hairs to ward off the effects of drying winds and to prevent water loss. The desert fuchsia *E. gilesii*, the grey-leafed form of *E. latrobei*, and *E. freelingii* with pale blue flowers can be seen growing on the hillsides near Alice Springs.

One of the joys of travelling by car (or even train) in inland Australia is the sight of colourful fields covered in wildflowers for as far as the eye can see. The colours and numbers vary in intensity according to rainfall, species and season, but after good rains the starkness of the desert can be softened and transformed into a beautiful glowing garden. These short-lived annuals are called ephemerals. Their tough-coated, drought-resistant seeds lie dormant, sometimes for many years, until heavy rains initiate germination. Within a few weeks of springing to life they flower briefly, go to seed and, as the plants die down, scatter their seeds and await the next rain.

One of the most spectacular of these annuals is the handsome Sturt's desert pea, *Clianthus formosus*, with its woolly, grey-green leaves and very showy, red, pea-shaped flowers with prominent bumps in the middle. It is named in honour of Charles Sturt, one of the most determined of Australian explorers and one who lived to tell the tale in two narratives of his explorations.

Should you travel all the way to Uluru (Ayers Rock) without seeing the Sturt's desert pea growing in its natural state don't be too disappointed. It is often cultivated at the Yulara Tourist Village and because of artificial watering may be in flower at any time. Spend some time at the village looking at some of the excellent examples of drought-resistant plants in cultivation. This can be especially useful for those with dry country gardens.

There are also informative daily botanical walks close to Uluru (Ayers Rock) which take in sandhill flora. Other botanical walks at the Olgas include the Olga Gorge and the Valley of the Winds.

If you have a four-wheel-drive vehicle or a day free for an organised tour take a trip to Palm Valley, a little west of Alice Springs. Visually and botanically it is a trip worth taking and one never to be forgotten. One gets the uncanny feeling of being in another age. The track on the way to Palm Valley follows the Finke River where wonderful river red gums provide welcome shade. Further along is the amphitheatre surrounded by high sandstone formations. Here there are some excellent examples of silver-grey vegetation typical of arid inland regions. A common plant well known in cultivation, the delightful silver cassia, can be seen here in its beautiful natural setting.

At Palm Valley the ancient *Livistonia mariae* palms are found. There are some 3000 established palms in this region growing in a narrow, rocky valley. On the surrounding chocolate-red cliffs fantastic ghost gums grow out of narrow crevices. Native pines, melaleucas and an interesting variety of smaller plants dot the surrounding landscape. There are also some excellent examples of the cycad *Macrozamia macdonnellii* which are often written about as being living fossils since their remains have been found along with those of dinosaurs.

In the sandplains and rocky hills around Alice Springs, spring is the best time to see many of the pretty flowering shrubs in blossom. These include a few different types of pussy tails, *Ptilotus* species, lots of wattles, pea flowers, eremophilas and bluebells. The aromatic mintbush, *Prostanthera striatiflora,* and the holly grevillea, *Grevillea wickhamii*, are found in rocky hills. Beside the road you might see growing the wild potato bush, *Solanum quadriloculatum*, a common tiny daisy plant, *Minuria leptophylla*, and the widespread parakeelya.

Within easy walking distance of Alice Springs is the Olive Pink Flora Reserve. A large part of the reserve takes in rocky hills which retain their original vegetation and the rest is devoted to the cultivation and preservation of species found within a radius of 200 km of Alice Springs.

Nullarbor Plain

If driving to Western Australia from the east you would have to travel across the Nullarbor Plain. The Nullarbor Plain extends across two States — South Australia and Western Australia. It is an extremely flat limestone plain and although its name is derived from the Latin *Nulla arbor* meaning no tree, only the central part of the plain is completely treeless. The highway passes close to the coast and only offers glimpses of a treeless plain; the rest is lightly wooded to varying degrees.

The Eyre Highway begins at Port Augusta, South Australia and leads directly to Norseman, Western Australia where you have to decide which route to take to Perth. The highway travels close to the coastline of the Great Australian Bight which provides some outstanding coastal scenery. From Port Augusta the road runs through lightly wooded areas and eucalypt scrublands known as mallee. Typical mallee species in the area are *Eucalyptus oleosa*, *E. dumosa* and *E. gracilis*. Good specimens of the white mallee, *E. gracilis*, can be seen from the road around Penong, South Australia.

The most conspicuous plant on the Nullarbor Plain is the bluebush, *Maireana sedifolia,* belonging to the Chenopodiaceae family which also includes saltbushes and samphires. It is a small shrub with silvery, succulent leaves and pale green to reddish fruit. It can be seen in both States and may either form part of an understorey beneath scrub or be scattered across the plains in the open. In drought times it might stand alone with bare pinkish-brown earth between, but in a good season it may form part of a rich groundcover of annual grasses, everlastings, Sturt's desert pea and numerous herbs.

The tree component is provided mainly by a few scattered small trees of myall, *Acacia papyrocarpa*, with its characteristic flat-top crown.

Gentle shallow depressions in plains tend to accumulate more moisture and show better growth. These occur frequently on the Nullarbor Plain and are known locally as dongas. They are recognisable by lusher plant growth which varies from perennial grasses or saltbushes to a few small trees such as myall, mulga, myoporum and *Pittosporum phylliraeoides*. After good rains a ground layer of ephemerals will bring bright colour to the area.

Western Australia

As you approach Belladonia, Western Australia the vegetation becomes more wooded with *Casuarina cristata*, mallees such as *Eucalyptus oleosa* and *E. flocktoniae,* and an understorey of cassias, eremophilas, bluebush and saltbush.

When you arrive at Norseman, Western Australia you will need to decide if you want to travel south to Perth via Esperance and Albany or north via Kalgoorlie. Botanically it is far more interesting to turn left and explore the South-west Province, but if you have time make a detour to Kalgoorlie. Kalgoorlie is a wonderful place to visit and if you are travelling with children it is an excellent and fun break for them after long days in the car.

On the way to Kalgoorlie you will get a taste of the botanical riches the west has to offer. The imposing salmon gums, *E. salmonophloia*, with their wonderful coloured trunks can be seen from the car and seem to be more outstanding north of Norseman even though a small town further south is called Salmon Gums. They often grow in association with the smaller growing gimlet, *E. salubris*, which is recognisable by its characteristic spirally-fluted trunks, particularly when young.

Not far from Coolgardie you will see the beautiful coral gum, *E. torquata*, growing on rocky soil on hillsides. It produces outstanding drooping bunches of pink flowers mostly in spring to summer, but as the tree is in bud for a long time, it is easily noticed in late winter by masses of red buds.

In Kalgoorlie when visiting places of interest, parks and even the streets you will notice some of the many outstanding species of small eucalypts with large showy flowers used in ornamental municipal plantings. Many of these are eucalypts of the Western Australian goldfields and include the yellow-green flowering *E. stricklandii*; *E. salubris* with colourful fluted trunks; *E. kruseana* noted for its opposite, rounded, grey leaves and yellow blossoms; *E. woodwardii* with frosted grey buds and lemon-yellow flowers; and the particularly successful street tree *E. torquata*.

On the road to Esperance look out for the small ornamental fuchsia gum *E. forrestiana* between Salmon Gums and Scadden. The one photographed in this book was found at Grass Patch. Also around Scadden and towards Esperance good examples of the frosted tallerack, *E. tetragona*, can be seen as well as a few specimens of the amazing straggly, square-fruited mallee, *E. tetraptera*, which often looks like it has fallen over or is about to fall over.

On reaching Esperance you will pass through some wonderful heathlands with a wealth of interesting and varied flora. The sensational *Banksia speciosa* is conspicuous with patches of smokebush, hakea, dryandra and isopogon. The red kangaroo paw is common in deep sandy areas.

From Esperance to Ravensthorpe you will pass through sandplains and heath. The turnoff to the botanically rich Fitzgerald River National Park is at Ravensthorpe. This park takes in an area between Bremer Bay and Hopetoun known in general as the Barren Ranges (small mountains divided into three groups which rise abruptly from platforms fronting on or near to the sea). The area is extremely well known for its wonderful plant life and is noted for a considerable number of species which do not occur elsewhere. The park's high floral diversity gives it the status of one of only two International Biosphere Reserves in Western Australia. It is truly a botanical wonderland well worth a visit. Plan ahead to maximise your time for plant browsing. The outstanding royal hakea, *Hakea victoria*, *Eucalyptus preissiana*, *Regelia velutina*, and

Dryandra quercifolia will be easily seen, but you will need to take your time to spot the lovely hidden flowers of the woolly banksia, *Banksia baueri*, the dainty trigger plants, fringe lilies, terrestrial orchids and the Qualup bell with its pendant, greenish-yellow flowers which might be missed if you are rushing.

The Stirling Range with its impressive landscape is noted for its wildflowers and challenging peaks. Bluff Knoll is the highest peak and is approached by a tourist road and then a walking trail to the summit. On the upper levels the vegetation is mostly a formation of dense thick scrub. Conspicuous species include *Isopogon latifolius*, *Dryandra formosa*, *Beaufortia decussata* and the very attractive red mountain pea, *Oxylobium atropurpureum*. Quite a number of pink-flowering boronias are found and there are eight endemic species of *Darwinia* found in the park. Growing on Bluff

Hovea elliptica (Tree hovea).
Karri forest, Pemberton, Western Australia.

Knoll are *D. collina* on the summit, *D. squarrosa* on the middle slopes and *D. lejostyla* on the lower slopes.

Patches of low woodland on the lower slopes of the range consist of jarrah and marri in a mallee heath formation. Here you will find a number of banksias, including interesting prostrate species; Drummond's wattle, *Acacia drummondii*; the Stirling Range coneflower, *Isopogon baxteri*; and a number of hakeas and dryandras. Many species of terrestrial orchids can be seen throughout the range.

Around Albany hundreds of different varieties of wildflowers can be found, such as melaleucas, bottlebrushes, kangaroo paws and banksias including the fabulous scarlet banksia, *B. coccinea,* and the red swamp banksia, *B. occidentalis*. In moist swampy areas near the coast grows the famous Albany pitcher plant, *Cephalotus follicularis*, an insectivorous plant found nowhere else in the world. Its swampy home makes it difficult to locate and it is best to ask a plant-interested local to show you.

On the southern coast between Albany and Denmark is West Cape Howe National Park with sandy beaches, coastal heaths and karri forest. The Albany pitcher plant is quite common on the edges of Lake William—one of the three fresh water lakes in the park. Also near to the lake a dense stand of the juniper myrtle or wattie, *Agonis juniperina*, can be seen. In spring the park becomes alive with colour with beautiful pea-flowering shrubs, wattles, melaleucas and pimeleas. In late summer the spectacular swamp bottlebrush, *Beaufortia sparsa*, blooms.

In the Pemberton–Northcliff area the traveller passes through giant karri forests which support a dense, tall-shrub understorey of karri oak, karri hazel and karri wattle. Where there is light and space, there are lower shrubs of some lovely blue-flowering species such as the tree hovea, dampieras and sarsaparilla, *Hardenbergia comptoniana*.

Although there is an extensive network of national parks and reserves fairly close to Perth a wonderful day can be spent observing wildflowers almost in the heart of the city at Kings Park. Approximately two-thirds of Kings Park is bushland which is a remnant of the original vegetation. There are numerous nature trails and beneath the jarrah, marri and tuart eucalypts one can find lovely drifts of fairy orchids, spider orchids and fringed lilies. Kangaroo paws are everywhere and so are many species of wattle and banksia. A botanic garden has been established in Kings Park. Although there are exotic species growing in the gardens from countries with a similar climate to that of Perth, the greater part of the garden is devoted to the flora of Western Australia and displays many of the beautiful flowering treasures the west has to offer.

North of Perth, the Mt Lesueur area east of Jurien Bay is one of the most botanically interesting areas in south-west Australia. The vegetation is mostly scrub heath on sandplains and is known locally as *kwongan,* an Aboriginal word in the south-western Nyungar language. Most of the shrubby species are less than one metre tall and are often studded with kingias towering above. Some wonderful species to be seen include the endemic pine banksia, *Banksia tricuspis*, one-sided bottlebrush, *Calothamnus quadrifidus*, staghorn bush, *Daviesia epiphylla*, and Lesueur hakea, *Hakea megalosperma*. Along the side of the road can be found species of *Conostylis*, kangaroo paws including the black kangaroo paw, smokebush and wattles.

Further north at the mouth of the Murchison River is the Kalbarri National Park. The vegetation is mainly *kwongan* and the area is famous for its wildflowers, many of which are unique to Kalbarri. A feature of the Kalbarri sandplains is *Grevillea leucopteris* which develops long floral branches held well above the bush. The flowers which appear throughout spring do, however, have an unpleasant odour. Outstanding colour effects are provided by the feather flowers, melaleucas, coppercups, smokebush and isopogon. The interesting sandplain woody pear, *Xylomelum angustifolium*, can be seen growing with the beautiful *Banksia sceptrum* in the park north of the Murchison River.

^ ^ ^

^^^ *White and Cream* ^^^

F·L·O·W·E·R·S

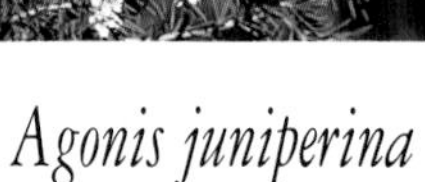

Agonis juniperina

^^^

JUNIPER MYRTLE, WATTIE
MYRTACEAE
WA

This species occurs mostly as a tall shrub to 3 m, but can reach tree-like proportions in forested habitats in south-west Western Australia. It has crowded, short, narrow leaves and tiny, white flowers grouped in rounded clusters towards the ends of branches during spring and autumn. This species is popular in cultivation and as it naturally occurs in moist situations will tolerate pooly drained soils. It is best suited to light shade.

Anthocercis viscosa

^^^

STICKY RAY-FLOWER
SOLANACEAE
WA

This attractive species can be seen growing in rocky crevices in southern coastal areas from Albany to Cape Arid, Western Australia. It is a sticky branched shrub to 3 m or more and has flat, obovate leaves to 6 cm long and 3 cm wide. The creamy-white, bell-shaped flowers with deeply cut lobes have greenish striations in the throat. The flowers are heavily perfumed and appear throughout the year.

Caladenia patersonii

^^^

COMMON SPIDER ORCHID
ORCHIDACEAE
WA, SA, QLD, NSW, VIC, TAS

This dainty terrestrial orchid is widespread in temperate Australia and can be seen as far north as the Murchison River, Western Australia. It often occurs in small clumps with a solitary hairy leaf up to 20 cm long. The erect flower stem to 40 cm tall carries up to four spider-like flowers. Flowers are white, greenish or deep pink and appear mostly in late winter and spring.

Clematis microphylla

^^^

SMALL-LEAFED CLEMATIS
RANUNCULACEAE
WA, SA, QLD, NSW, VIC

This widespread species occurs mostly in dryish areas but can also be found on coastal sand dunes. It is a dainty climber which will lightly scramble over nearby plants. The leaves are composed of three leaflets up to 3 cm long. Loose clusters of greenish-white flowers are produced in the upper leaf axils in late winter and spring. These are followed by conspicuous balls of fluffy, white seed heads.

Conospermum stoechadis

^^^

COMMON SMOKEBUSH
PROTEACEAE
WA

This delightful wildflower of the sand-heaths is widespread in the south-west and also occurs inland to Southern Cross. It is an upright, many-stemmed, rounded shrub to 2 m tall and has terete leaves to 15 cm long. The tiny, woolly, tubular flowers are borne on slender stems in spring. They are greyish-white in colour and when seen from a distance resemble smoke, from which many of the species have gained the common name of smokebush.

Conostephium pendulum

^^^

PEARL FLOWER
EPACRIDACEAE
WA

This small plant occurs in coastal areas around Perth and is quite common in Kings Park. It is an erect shrub to around 50 cm tall. The linear leaves to 3 cm long, have rolled margins and end with a sharp point. Pendulous, white, tubular flowers to 2 cm long have a purple tip. These have a long flowering season and can be seen during winter and spring.

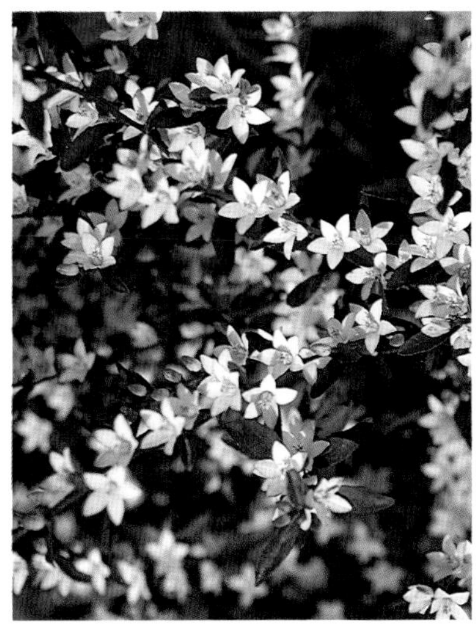

Crowea angustifolia

^^^

RUTACEAE
WA

Of the three species of *Crowea* only one is found in Western Australia. There are two forms: *C. angustifolia* var. *angustifolia* found in moist swamp areas grows to around 60 cm with linear leaves to 5 cm long and has pink, star-like flowers while *C. angustifolia* var. *dentata* occurs in karri forests, may reach 3 m in height and has obovate leaves. The flowers are usually white. Both flower in late winter and early spring.

Dasypogon bromeliifolius

^^^

PINEAPPLE-LEAVED DASYPOGON
XANTHORRHOEACEAE
WA

This low, clump-forming perennial is common on sandy soils of the southern coastal plains and the jarrah forests. It has lightly-toothed, grass-like leaves to 30 cm long which taper to a point. The terminal creamy-white, rounded flower heads, on stems to 40 cm high, are held well above the arching foliage. They are produced from late winter to early summer.

Eremophila bignoniiflora

^^^

BIGNONIA EMU-BUSH, EURAH

MYOPORACEAE

ALL MAINLAND STATES

A shrub or small tree from 2 to 7 m high with a wide inland distribution inhabits areas subject to periodic flooding. It forms a leafy, rounded crown with drooping foliage. The light green, narrow leaves up to 18 cm long taper to a point. Cream-coloured, tubular flowers with rounded lobes have a purplish flecked interior. They are lightly fragrant and are produced during the cooler months. The succulent oval fruits are eaten by emus.

Eucalyptus flocktoniae

^^^

MERRIT

MYRTACEAE

WA, SA

This slender, smooth-barked tree or sometimes a mallee, up to 12 m high, occurs in the Eyre Peninsula, South Australia and over a large range in the south-west of Western Australia. It has dark green, lanceolate leaves to 11 cm long with noticeable oil glands. Pendulous flower buds with a beaked cap are slightly wider than the base. There may be up to eleven in a cluster of creamy-white flowers. Flowers are produced mainly during spring, but can also be seen at other times. Pendulous small urn-shaped fruits follow.

Eucalyptus incrassata

^^^

LERP MALLEE
MYRTACEAE
WA, SA, NSW, VIC

The lerp mallee has a wide distribution across southern Australia where it occurs in semi-arid areas; often near the coast of South Australia to just north of Perth, Western Australia. It grows to around 5 m high and has smooth, grey-brown bark which sheds in ribbons in late summer. The thick, glossy, lanceolate leaves are up to 11 cm long. Flower buds have a beaked cap and a slightly ribbed base. Creamy-white or pale yellow flowers appear mostly during spring followed by small, urn-shaped fruits. This attractive species is best suited to gardens with low rainfall and will grow in well-drained soils.

Eucalyptus oldfieldii

^^^

OLDFIELD'S MALLEE
MYRTACEAE
WA

A most attractive widespread mallee found in sandy heaths in temperate and semi-arid regions of Western Australia. It grows to around 8 m tall with deciduous, grey-brown bark and reddish young branchlets. The thick, grey-green, lanceolate to ovate leaves to 10 cm have visible lateral veins. Cup-shaped flower buds in threes have beaked caps. Creamy-white flowers, up to 2 cm across, appear in masses during spring, followed by cup-shaped fruits with large raised valves.

Eucalyptus tetragona

^^^

Tallerack
Myrtaceae
WA

This silvery mallee occurs often in the southern sandy heaths of Western Australia and is often found near the coast. It is a straggly mallee or small tree to 8 m high. Stems, leaf blades, flower buds and fruits have a white, frosted coating. The grey-green, oval leaves to 15 cm are on thick stalks which extend onto a four-angled stem. The four-sided flower buds, in threes, have rounded caps. Showy, creamy-white flowers appear in late spring and summer followed by four-sided grey fruits. This species is best suited to low rainfall areas and may be grown near the coast with some protection.

Grevillea crithmifolia

^^^

Proteaceae
WA

This spreading shrub of variable height up to 2 m grows naturally around Perth on sandy, coastal soils. It has grey-green leaves divided into narrow leaflets and bears masses of creamy-white flowers from pinkish buds during winter and spring. The prostrate form of this plant is popular in cultivation as a rockery and groundcover plant. It is hardy and adaptable and will do well in most well-drained situations.

Grevillea endlicheriana

^^^

SPINDLY GREVILLEA
PROTEACEAE
WA

This tall, dense shrub with rather slender branches occurs on granite slopes on the Darling Scarp. It has narrow, silky leaves up to 13 cm and clusters of creamy-white flowers on long, almost leafless branches mostly during the winter and spring months. In cultivation this fast growing species can be grown in coastal areas with some protection and will tolerate dry periods. Provide good drainage and prune to shape.

Grevillea intricata

^^^

PROTEACEAE
WA

This attractive, many-branched shrub to 3 m tall occurs in granite country around the Murchison River area. It has terete leaves divided into three narrow segments ending with pointed tips. The creamy, toothbrush-like flowers are produced in profusion during winter and spring. This is a good, fast growing shrub for dry country gardens and is useful as a privacy screen, hedge or windbreak. It can be kept very compact by persistent pruning.

Grevillea leucopteris

^^^

WHITE-PLUMED GREVILLEA

PROTEACEAE

WA

This conspicuous shrub of the sandplains and heathlands north of Perth bears large clusters of creamy flowers on long, leafless branches held well above its foliage. It is a dense, rounded shrub with grey-green, ferny leaves with soft, hairy segments. The flowers which have a strong unpleasant odour appear in spring and summer and are pollinated by night flying moths. This dry area grevillea can be successfully grown in semi-arid gardens if drainage is good.

Grevillea uncinulata

^^^

PROTEACEAE

WA

This extremely beautiful flowering shrub occurs in the drier parts of the south-west of Western Australia in sandy soils. It is a small, hairy shrub to around 1 m high with dark green, linear leaves to 1.5 cm with a silky undersurface. They are crowded in groups along the branches and end with a small curved point. The profuse, creamy-white, woolly flowers with hairy styles have bright yellow and orange tips. Flowers appear throughout winter to mid spring.

Hakea lissocarpha

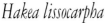

^^^

HONEYBUSH
PROTEACEAE
WA

A small shrub to 1 m high with numerous spreading branches found growing in a number of habitats over a wide area of south-west Western Australia. The rigid, terete leaves are divided and end with a sharp point. The numerous, sweetly-scented flowers are usually white but may be tinged pink. They are produced mostly from late autumn and during winter. This interesting, bird attracting, garden plant will do well in a wide range of climatic conditions and well-drained soils.

Hakea nitida

^^^

FROG HAKEA, SHINING HAKEA
PROTEACEAE
WA

This vigorous, multi-branched shrub from 1 to 3 m tall has forms that can vary in size and leaf shape. It occurs in the southern sandplains of the Eyre district. The leaves are thick, smooth, about 10 cm long, entire or irregularly toothed and tapering to the stem. Flowers are in dense clusters, cream-coloured and usually produced in profusion during the winter months. Attractive swollen, oval fruit to 4 cm long have two horns at the tip and dark brown spots. In the garden provide lots of sun and good drainage.

Hakea suaveolens

^^^

SWEET-SCENTED HAKEA
PROTEACEAE
WA

This erect round shrub to 3 m or more high is usually found on granite hills close to the coast of southern Western Australia. It has stiff, terete, often divided leaves and bears numerous small, white, scented flowers in dense clusters in the upper axils mostly during autumn and winter. This hardy shrub is adaptable to varying soil types and conditions provided drainage is good. In South Africa and New Zealand it has become naturalised and is considered a noxious weed.

Hakea suberea

^^^

CORKBARK
PROTEACEAE
WA, NT

This small, gnarled tree to 6 m high is common inland among rocks and on ridges. Its trunk is often twisted and is covered in thick, deeply-cleft bark. The needle-like, grey-green leaves may be up to 30 cm long. Spikes of pale cream to greenish-yellow flowers are produced mostly during autumn and winter. There are beautiful examples of this hakea in the hills just north of Alice Springs. It is well suited to dry inland gardens where it requires a sunny, well-drained position.

Kingia australis

^^^

GRASSTREE, BLACK GIN
XANTHORRHOEACEAE
WA

This marvellous feature plant of south-west Western Australia is common between Perth and Albany. It may reach up to 5 m tall, has a single rough trunk and a dense crown of long, stiff leaves up to 1 m long. The silky, rounded flower heads are produced at the end of long stalks which arise from the top of the plant.

Lachnostachys eriobotrya

^^^

LAMBSWOOL
CHLOANTHACEAE
WA

This grey, spreading shrub to 1.5 m tall is common in the sandplains and heath north of Perth to Northampton. The whole of the plant is covered with soft, dense wool. It has linear leaves to 4 cm long and loose panicles of white, felted flowers with violet stamens in late winter and early spring.

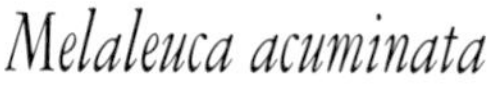

Melaleuca acuminata

^^^

CREAMY HONEY MYRTLE
MYRTACEAE
WA, SA, VIC

A widespread species found in forested habitats in drier regions usually as an understorey plant. It is a branched, upright shrub to around 2 m tall with small, opposite, lanceolate leaves. The numerous creamy-white flowers are borne in sessile clusters, forming dense, uninterrupted, cylindrical spikes around the previous year's wood. They have a light vanilla fragrance.

Melaleuca hamulosa

^^^

MYRTACEAE
WA, SA

A tall, slender, upright shrub to 3 m or more high which occurs in the drier inland parts of southern Western Australia and South Australia. It has alternate, fine, crowded leaves to no more than 2 cm long ending with a hooked tip. The white or pale pink flowers are crowded in dense cylindrical spikes to 4 cm long. They appear mostly during spring and early summer.

Melaleuca incana

^^^

GREY HONEY MYRTLE
MYRTACEAE
WA

This very popular garden subject grows naturally on wet or swampy land in the Stirling, Warren and Darling districts in south-west Western Australia. It is a soft, woolly shrub or small tree to 3 m tall with spreading or weeping branches. The pubescent, grey-green linear leaves are either irregularly scattered or can be in whorls of threes. The numerous creamy brushes of flowers appear in mid spring followed by dense cylindrical spikes of woody capsules. It needs a well-drained position in the garden, but must not be allowed to dry out when young.

Melaleuca viminea

^^^

MYRTACEAE
WA

This dense, rounded shrub to 2.5 m tall with branches almost to the ground frequents swampy soil in south-west Western Australia. It has narrow, linear leaves to around 12 mm long with recurved tips. The creamy-white flowers are carried in short, elongated, terminal spikes during late spring and early summer. In the garden provide a sunny, open position and plenty of moisture during dry periods.

Minuria leptophylla

^^^

MINNIE DAISY

ASTERACEAE

ALL MAINLAND STATES

This dwarf, rounded plant is common throughout the drier regions and is found in a variety of habitats and soils. It grows to around 20 cm high and has bright green, narrow leaves to 2.5 cm long. Masses of small, daisy-like flowers are produced in profusion throughout the year with a main flush in spring. Flowers are white or in shades of mauve and pink.

Myoporum acuminatum

^^^

DESERT BOOBIALLA

MYOPORACEAE

ALL MAINLAND STATES

A widespread species found in drier inland areas usually on sandy and rocky soils. It is a multi-branched, dense shrub up to 3 m high with light green, lanceolate leaves up to 14 cm long. The small, well-shaped, white flowers in groups of up to five, have a bearded interior with purple spots. They are produced mostly in late winter and spring followed by rounded, white to purple fruit. This is a hardy, drought-resistant shrub for inland gardens.

Myoporum parvifolium

^^^

Creeping boobialla
Myoporaceae
WA, NT, SA, Vic

A low spreading shrub to 1 m across usually found close to the sea, often in saline situations. It has fleshy oblong leaves to 3 cm long and numerous white, star-shaped flowers with a purple dotted interior. These are produced in spring and summer, followed by rounded purplish fruit. This very pretty groundcover is quite often available from general nurseries. It is drought and frost resistant and can be grown in seaside gardens.

Myriocephalus stuartii

^^^

Poached eggs
Asteraceae
NT, SA, Qld, NSW, Vic

This delightful wildflower of the inland occurs mostly on sandplains and dunes and often forms spectacular yellow and white carpets over vast areas. It is an erect, woolly annual to 50 cm high and has woolly, light green leaves to 7 cm long. The white, papery flowers have bright yellow centres mostly in late winter and spring. Packets of seeds can be bought in some nurseries. They are best sown in autumn and do best in semi-arid gardens.

Olearia pimeleoides

^^^

BURROBUNGA

ASTERACEAE

WA, SA, QLD, NSW, VIC

This most attractive shrub is common in dry inland areas. It is a rounded, woolly shrub to 1 m high with small, greyish, obovate leaves to 1 cm long with a woolly undersurface. The conspicuous, white, daisy-like flowers are produced singly at the ends of the branches during spring.

Olearia rudis

^^^

ROUGH DAISY BUSH

ASTERACEAE

WA, SA, NSW, VIC

This very pretty, small shrub is widespread in the southern regions of Australia. It grows to 1 m tall with stem-clasping, obovate leaves with serrated margins to 4 cm long. The showy, daisy-like flowers up to 4 cm across are usually borne singly. They vary in colour from white to pale blue or mauve and are produced in winter and spring.

Prostanthera striatiflora

^^^

STREAKED MINT BUSH
LAMIACEAE
WA, NT, SA, QLD, NSW

This shrub occurs in dry inland areas often in sandy soils and rocky outcrops. It is a bushy shrub to 2 m with stem-clasping, pale green, lanceolate leaves which are strongly fragrant when rubbed. Abundant, large, creamy-white, tubular flowers with prominent purple striations in the throat are produced mostly in late spring and summer. This is a beautiful plant best suited to dry inland gardens where it requires very good drainage and a light soil. Tip pruning should be carried out throughout the life of the plant.

Stylidium crossocephalum

^^^

POSY TRIGGERPLANT
STYLIDIACEAE
WA

This wonderful tiny plant grows to only 20 cm high when it is flowering and is rather difficult to spot in its sandheath habitat. It is an erect, grass-like plant with narrow, linear leaves to 10 cm long. The small, white flowers with red, papery bracts are produced in terminal clusters during spring.

Verticordia huegelii

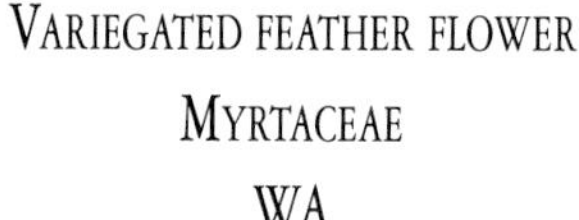

^^^

VARIEGATED FEATHER FLOWER

MYRTACEAE

WA

This low spreading, small shrub to 50 cm high grows on a variety of soils and can be seen in the granite foothills east of Perth. It has small, bluish-green, semi-terete leaves and bears masses of heavily fringed, creamy-white flowers that deepen to a pretty rose colour with age. These are produced during spring.

Xanthosia rotundifolia

^^^

SOUTHERN CROSS

APIACEAE

WA

This pretty wildflower, common in southern coastal areas of Western Australia, gets its common name from the cross-like formation of the flowers. It is a low spreading perennial to 50 cm high with fleshy, ovate leaves with toothed margins. The small, creamy-white flowers have large bracts and are produced throughout the year with a good showing in spring.

Yellow

F·L·O·W·E·R·S

Abutilon leucopetalum

^^^

Common lantern bush
Malvaceae
WA, SA, NT, Qld

This small, spreading, tomentose shrub to around 1 m high is frequently found in inland areas on skeletal soils and rocky hills. The soft, oval, heart-shaped leaves have toothed edges. Small hibiscus-like flowers to 4 cm across are mostly bright yellow in colour although white forms can be found. These are produced during autumn and winter. Abutilons are found in warmer regions of the world and a number are cultivated for their lovely drooping, lantern-like flowers. This species is quite ornamental and is best suited to inland gardens with good drainage.

Acacia alata

^^^

Winged wattle
Mimosaceae
WA

This unusual small shrub with many branches grows to around 1 m or more high. It is found near creeks in shady, forested areas in the south-west of Western Australia. The leaves form part of the flattened, zig-zagging, hairy stems. They are triangular in shape and taper into a sharp point. The cream or bright yellow flower heads in ones or twos are produced from the axils. In cultivation this species does best in semi-shade and is ideal for growing under taller shrubs and trees.

Acacia aneura

^^^

Mulga
Mimosaceae
WA, SA, NT, Qld, NSW

Mulga is widely distributed over the arid areas of inland Australia and is commonly found in red, sandy soil. It is a variable bushy shrub or small tree up to 10 m tall. The grey-green phyllodes are variable in shape and size from very narrow to oblong and flat, and are covered in minute, short hairs. The bright yellow flower spikes on stalks up to 1 cm long are produced at irregular periods throughout the year, usually after good summer rains. Thin oblong pods may follow if rainfall is adequate. This is a good drought-resistant species for hot dry inland gardens.

Acacia dictyophleba

^^^

Mimosaceae
WA, SA, NT, Qld

A resinous shrub from 1 to 4 m high found inland on desert dunes and open woodland. The sticky phyllodes up to 7 cm long are oblanceolate or narrow-elliptic, ending with a small, pointed tip. Bright yellow flower balls, either singly or in pairs, are carried on 2 cm stalks during autumn and winter. Oblong pods to 9 cm long often have a shiny varnished appearance. A good ornamental and drought tolerant species for inland gardens.

Acacia drummondii

^^^

DRUMMOND'S WATTLE
MIMOSACEAE
WA

When in bloom this very pretty, ferny-leafed wattle is a conspicuous understorey shrub in the forests of south-west Western Australia. It may reach 2 m in height but is extremely variable and low growing forms, including a prostrate form, can be seen. It has thin, reddish branches and finely divided leaves. Large, bright yellow flower spikes on longish stalks are produced during spring. This is an extremely ornamental plant for the garden. It enjoys a sheltered, well-drained position.

Acacia extensa

^^^

WIRY WATTLE
MIMOSACEAE
WA

This easy to recognise wattle is distinguished by its very long, terete leaves to 20 cm which are very similar to its thin, wiry branches. It grows to around 3 m high and is found in moist sites in jarrah forests of the south-west of Western Australia. Masses of yellow, ball flowers are borne along the stem in late winter and spring. A pretty free flowering and adaptable shrub for the garden where it will do best in a partially shaded moist, but well-drained position.

Acacia georginae

^^^

Gidgee, Gidyea
Mimosaceae
NT, Qld

This small spreading tree to around 5 m high grows on floodplains in dry inland areas. It has grey-green, linear-lanceolate phyllodes to 8 cm long ending with a small point. Profuse yellow flower balls are borne in clusters along branch ends during winter and spring. When brushed against or after a shower of rain, the phyllodes and flowers give off a very unpleasant odour which makes this otherwise attractive plant unsuitable for planting in parks or near the house. It is known to be extremely poisonous to stock.

Acacia glaucoptera

^^^

Clay wattle, Flat wattle
Mimosaceae
WA

This attractive and interesting wattle is quite common in the south-west of Western Australia from the Stirling Ranges to Esperance. It can be found in heathlands or mallee shrubs. It has flattened, wavy stems and flat, wing-like, triangular leaves along the stems. The leaves are blue-green and narrow into a sharp point. Brightly coloured new growth is often an attractive bronze-red. Bright yellow, rounded flower heads are borne from nodes on the phylodes in late winter and spring. This wattle has adapted to cultivation, where it prefers part shade and good drainage.

Acacia hakeoides

^^^

Hakea wattle
Mimosaceae
WA, SA, Qld, NSW, Vic

A bushy, spreading shrub up to 4 m high found in drier parts mainly in open scrub. The phylodes are narrow, leathery and are widest at the tip. They are variable and range from 4 to 12 cm in length. The bright yellow flowers are carried in dense sprays of up to twelve flowers mostly during winter and early spring. This is a reliable ornamental plant for inland gardens where it will withstand dry periods and frost.

Acacia merrallii

^^^

Merrall's wattle
Mimosaceae
WA, SA

A small bushy shrub to around 1 m high with a wider spread. It is found near coastal areas in the Nullarbor region and southern areas of Western Australia. The slightly angular pubescent branches carry broad, ovate, greyish phyllodes about 2 cm long, ending in a sharp curved point. Flower buds are tinged pink. Numerous, but small, yellow flower balls are produced on long, slender stalks during spring. Attractive, loosely coiled pods follow. In the garden provide good drainage and an open sunny position.

Acacia saligna

^^^

Golden wreath wattle
Mimosaceae
WA

A dense, bushy shrub or small tree to 5 m or more high. It has attractive pendulous branches and linear to lanceolate, grey-green phyllodes up to 30 cm long with a prominent mid-vein. Long dense clusters of golden ball flowers are produced in profusion during spring and early summer. Long flat pods to 15 cm long are slightly constricted between seeds. This spectacular flowering species is well known to cultivation and is a hardy and adaptable ornamental shade tree.

Adenanthos detmoldii

^^^

Proteacaea
WA

An erect shrub to 4 m high found in sandy and moist spots in the south-west. It has linear, glandular leaves to 8 cm long which are hairy when young. Throughout the winter months it bears attractive yellow flowers with an orange throat and protruding styles. This decorative species is best grown in areas with low humidity.

Anigozanthos flavidus

^^^

TALL KANGAROO PAW
HAEMODORACEAE
WA

This tall growing species is commonly found in moist or swampy areas of forested regions from around Albany to Busselton. It forms large perennial clumps up to 3 m tall when in flower. The smooth, strap-like leaves may have marginal hairs in young plants. Tall, branched flower stems produce numerous pale greenish-yellow flowers during the spring months. Some forms with rusty-red flowers can also be seen. This species is the most successful in cultivation outside Western Australia and has become an important cut-flower both in Australia and overseas.

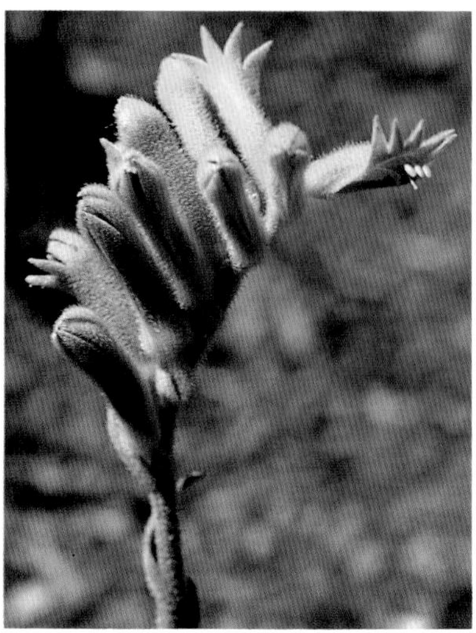

Anigozanthos humilis

^^^

CAT'S PAW
HAEMODORACEAE
WA

This small growing species to 20 cm high is the smallest of the paws. It is widely distributed in the south-west and always occurs on sandy soils. The velvety, tubular flowers are produced mainly on a single flower stem and are usually yellow suffused with red or salmon. They bloom for a long period during winter and spring. Grow this small plant in a container or sunny rockery pocket where its charming flowers can be displayed to advantage.

Anigozanthos pulcherrimus

^^^

YELLOW KANGAROO PAW
HAEMODORACEAE
WA

This species occurs on sandplains north of Perth to the Shark Bay area and to around 100 km inland. It is a clump forming perennial with flat, greyish leaves clothed with matted dense hairs and branched flowering stems up to 1.5 m tall. The striking golden-yellow flowers appear from November to February. A showy plant for the garden where it requires a sunny, well-drained position.

Banksia baxteri

^^^

BIRD'S-NEST BANKSIA
PROTEACEAE
WA

This open, spreading shrub is common in the southern coastal heaths between Albany and Hopetoun. It grows up to 4 m high and has ornamental prickly leaves that are divided to the mid-rib into triangular lobes. The dome-shaped, yellowish-green flowers are set in a rosette of new leaves. The spent, withered, grey flowers persist on the cones giving the appearance of a bird's nest. This is a most attractive and adaptable shrub for the garden. Provide good drainage and full sun.

Banksia speciosa

^^^

SHOWY BANKSIA
PROTEACEAE
WA

An outstanding plant of the coastal sandy heaths of Western Australia where it can sometimes be seen in large spectacular stands. It is a large, open shrub to 5 m with white, woolly branches and wonderful long, dark-green leaves to 40 cm with triangular lobes and a white, felty undersurface. The large flower spikes begin life as grey buds with yellow stamens opening from the bottom upwards. Flowers appear mainly in summer and autumn. This is a reliable plant for growing in protected coastal gardens.

Caladenia flava

^^^

COWSLIP ORCHID
ORCHIDACEAE
WA

This bright yellow ground orchid is common in the south-west of Western Australia and usually occurs in sandy soils. The flowers are 4 cm or more across and up to four may be found on one stem. The red markings on the labellum are variable. The plants are usually less than 25 cm high. The cowslip orchid has not proved successful in cultivation.

Cassia artemisioides

^^^

SILVER CASSIA
CAESALPINIACEAE
WA, SA, NT, NSW

Although an inhabitant of dry inland areas, this cassia has adapted very well to cultivation and is hardy in areas with extreme dryness, frosts and some coastal exposure. It is a neat, rounded shrub to 2 m with attractive silvery-grey pinnate leaves with up to eight pairs of narrow leaflets. The whole of the plant is covered in fine silky hairs. Bright yellow buttercup flowers are produced in loose sprays from spring through to autumn.

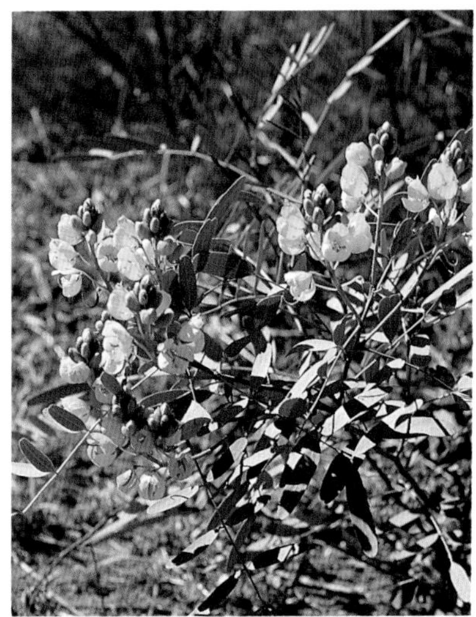

Cassia nemophila

^^^

DESERT CASSIA
CAESALPINIACEAE
WA, SA, NT, NSW, VIC

This widespread cassia is common on sandy soils in inland areas and is extremely variable in leaf form. Several different varieties and some natural hybrids are known, making identification often very difficult. It is a slender, erect shrub 1 to 3 m tall with leaves up to 8 cm long which may be composed of one or more pairs of leaflets. Bright yellow flowers in groups of three to ten are produced in winter and spring. Some varieties of this cassia are known in cultivation and are ideal for hot inland gardens where they will withstand periods of dryness. Previously known as *C. eremophila*.

Cassia venusta

^^^

CAESALPINIACEAE

WA, NT, QLD

An erect spreading shrub to 2 m high. New growth is softly pubescent. The grey-green leaves to 25 cm long are composed of six to fifteen pairs of oblong leaflets. Numerous yellow flowers are borne in long sprays at the ends of erect branches mostly during spring. This attractive, large-flowered species can be seen around Alice Springs as well as northern coastal areas. It would make a colourful display in warm inland or tropical gardens.

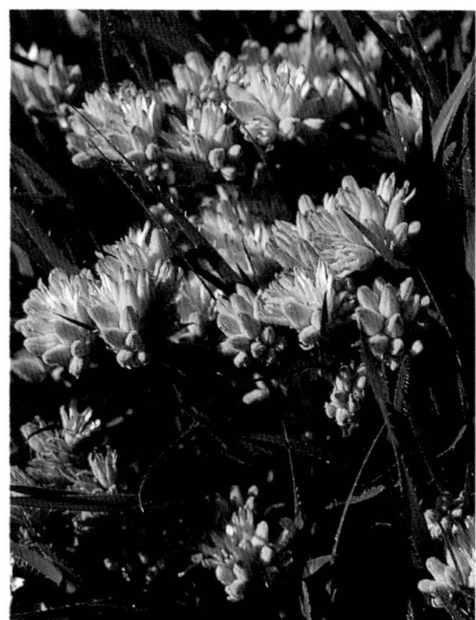

Conostylis aculeata

^^^

HAEMODORACEAE

WA

A perennial clumping plant with strap-like leaves up to 35 cm long. The leaves vary considerably and may have bristly spines along the margins or only towards the tips. The woolly, yellow flowers are borne in dense globular heads on stems that are often shorter than the leaves. This is an extremely attractive small plant for the garden or containers. It does best in a well-drained, light, sandy soil.

Conostylis candicans

^^^

GREY COTTONHEADS
HAEMODORACEAE
WA

A small tufted plant to 50 cm high with slender, grey, felted leaves to 50 cm long. The hairy yellow flowers form a rounded head on branched stems that are longer than the leaves. A common plant in coastal areas of south-west Western Australia. This is an attractive silvery plant for a well-drained, sunny, rockery pocket.

Conostylis prolifera

^^^

MAT COTTONHEADS
HAEMODORACEAE
WA

This is a low growing, tufted plant to around 30 cm high that may form dense carpeting mats. The soft, fine, green leaves to 10 cm are often edged with small bristles. Flower stems are longer than the leaves. Each flower is 1.2 cm long, pale yellow and hairy on the outside. This species is common on sandheaths and damp places in forested areas. In the garden it prefers some shade and a moist, but well-drained soil.

Conostylis robusta

^^^

HAEMODORACEAE
WA

This tough perennial forms clumps up to 45 cm high. The leaves to 45 cm long, are edged with small spines. The deep yellow, tubular flowers form dense, rounded heads on stems held well above the foliage in spring and summer. This is an adaptable plant for the garden suited to good drainage, full sun or part shade.

Conostylis seorsiflora

^^^

HAEMODORACEAE
WA

A prostrate, mat forming plant with a suckering habit. It has very narrow, flat leaves to around 15 cm long. The solitary, yellow, star-like flowers are hairy on the outside. They are borne on short stems mostly during spring. This is a popular rockery plant that can be found at nurseries selling native plants. Provide good drainage and a little shade for best results.

Conothamnus aureus

^^^

MYRTACEAE

WA

A small, many-stemmed, dome-shaped shrub to around 30 cm high. It has ovate, hairy leaves to about 1 cm. The golden-yellow flowers in fluffy, rounded heads are produced at the ends of the branches and are very prolific in spring. This species occurs naturally on deep sandy soil and requires excellent drainage in cultivation.

Diuris longifolia

^^^

COMMON DONKEY ORCHID

ORCHIDACEAE

WA, SA, NSW, VIC, TAS

This widespread terrestrial orchid is found over much of southern Australia in a variety of habitats. It grows up to 50 cm high and has up to three slender, channelled leaves per plant. The delightful yellow flowers suffused with brown are varied on slender stems to 50 cm tall. There may be up to eight flowers per stem. This is one of the easiest of the terrestrial orchids to grow. For information on obtaining tubers contact your local Native Orchid Society.

Dryandra ashbyi

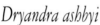

^^^

PROTEACEAE
WA

This highly ornamental erect shrub to 2.5 m high is found in the Geraldton area growing on gravelly hills. It has blue-green or dark green leaves to 8 cm long with widely spaced, pungent lobes. The bright yellow flower heads up to 4 cm across are borne on short side branches in profusion during late autumn and winter. This species is uncommon in cultivation.

Dryandra praemorsa

^^^

CUT-LEAF DRYANDRA
PROTEACEAE
WA

This attractive bushy shrub to 2 m or more high occurs in the jarrah forest of the Darling District east of Perth. It has stiff, prickly leaves cut short at the tip, with a white undersurface. The foliage forms a rosette around large, yellow flowers up to 8 cm across. These are produced at the ends of short branches during winter and spring. This outstanding dryandra is sometimes available from nurseries specialising in native plants. It requires excellent drainage and a partly shaded position.

Dryandra quercifolia

^^^

OAK-LEAF DRYANDRA
PROTEACEAE
WA

This outstanding flowering shrub occurs on a variety of gravelly soils between the Fitzgerald River and Ravensthorpe. It will reach up to 2 m or more high and has densely hairy branches. The prickly, lobed leaves are up to 9 cm long. Yellow flowers up to 6 cm across with prominent brown bracts are surrounded by a rosette of floral leaves. Flowers appear mostly during autumn and winter. This species is one of the best in cultivation. It will grow in a variety of well-drained soils and in dry situations if additional water is supplied.

Dryandra sessilis

^^^

PARROT BUSH
PROTEACEAE
WA

This showy, tall shrub to 6 m high has prickly, holly-like, grey-green leaves and bears abundant yellowish-green flowers in heads surrounded by floral leaves. It is common in jarrah forests and can be found along the coast from Geraldton to Esperance on the south coast of Western Australia. This species is popular in cultivation and has proved adaptable in a variety of soils providing the drainage is good. Flowers appear in winter and spring.

Eucalyptus grossa

^^^

COARSE-LEAVED MALLEE

MYRTACEAE

WA

This spreading mallee or small, straggly tree to 6 m high occurs inland from south of Norseman across to Belladonia with an occurrence around the Hopetoun area. It has smooth, reddish branches and thick, glossy, dark green, ovate leaves to 13 cm long with a distinct mid-rib and marginal vein. The brownish-red, bullet-shaped flower buds, in groups of up to seven, open to release bright yellowish-green filaments. Flowers are at their best during the spring months. This is an adaptable species for warm and dry inland gardens.

Eucalyptus preissiana

^^^

BELL-FRUITED MALLEE

MYRTACEAE

WA

An eyecatching mallee found in the Stirling Range eastward to around Esperance where it occurs near the coast. It grows to around 3 m or more high and has thick, ovate, grey-green leaves up to 12 cm long. The reddish, pear-shaped flower buds, in threes, are borne on a flattened peduncle. Conspicuous bright yellow flowers occur mainly in winter and spring. The ornate, bell-shaped fruits are numerous on the old wood. An adaptable and ornamental species which has been successfully cultivated in areas with low humidity. Good drainage is important.

Eucalyptus woodwardii

^^^

LEMON-FLOWERED GUM
MYRTACEAE
WA

This ornamental tree is often seen cultivated as a street and park tree in arid and semi-arid cities and towns in southern Australia. However, it has a restricted natural occurrence in an area around 100 km east of Kalgoorlie. It grows to around 12 m high with smooth, pale, deciduous bark and a broad crown of alternate, thick, grey-green, lanceolate leaves to 15 cm long. Stems, flower buds and fruits have a whitish, frosted appearance. It has faintly ribbed flower buds in umbels of up to seven and wonderful bright yellow flowers in winter and spring. Bell-shaped fruits up to 1.5 cm long follow.

Eutaxia obovata

^^^

FABACEAE
WA

This small, spreading shrub occurs in coastal heaths and karri forests in southern Western Australia. It reaches around 1.5 m high with slender, twiggy branches densely covered with obovate-oblong, grey-green leaves which end in a short point. From the axils of the leaves masses of bright yellow and red pea flowers are produced towards branch ends. Flowers appear throughout spring. This colourful and reliable species has become very popular in cultivation. It does well in most well-drained soils in a partly shaded position.

Ficus platypoda

^^^

ROCK FIG

MORACEAE

WA, NT, QLD, NSW

This is a large branched shrub or small tree to around 8 m often seen growing over rocky surfaces in very exposed positions. The specimen photographed was growing out of a narrow crevice quite a distance from the ground on Ayers Rock. The leathery leaves to 12 cm long can be elliptic, ovate to lanceolate. The rounded receptacles, to 1.5 cm across, are yellow-green but darken to orange-red with age. They ripen during autumn and winter. This is a good shade tree for dry inland gardens if extra water can be provided during long dry spells.

Goodenia affinis

^^^

CUSHION GOODENIA

GOODENIACEAE

WA, SA

This small, felted perennial herb is found growing on sandy plains on the coast or inland over a wide range of southern Australia. It forms a rosette of oblanceolate, grey-green leaves that are covered with fine woolly hairs. The margins may be faintly toothed. The bright yellow flowers up to 2 cm across are carried singly on a long stalk, sometimes longer than the foliage. Many flowers are produced during spring and summer.

Goodenia cycloptera

^^^

SERRATED GOODENIA
GOODENIACEAE
WA, SA, NT, QLD, NSW

This mat forming, perennial plant of Central Australia is usually found on sandy and gravelly soils. It has soft, pubescent, spreading stems and felted, oblong to obovate leaves to 7 cm long, which may be coarsely toothed or slightly lobed. The solitary yellow flowers, with broadly winged lobes, to 2 cm across, are carried on stems often longer than the leaves. Numerous flowers appear during the spring months.

Goodenia grandiflora

^^^

LARGE-FLOWERED GOODENIA
GOODENIACEAE
WA, NT, SA, QLD, NSW

A small, erect variable plant with a wide distribution and a variety of habitats. It has angular stems and leaves may be ovate to orbicular with toothed margins and pointed tip. Flowers to around 3 cm across may be solitary or in threes. They are usually yellow with purple striations, but blue, pink and white flowering forms can also be seen. Flowers appear from late winter to early summer.

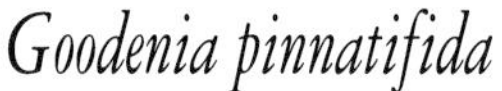

Goodenia pinnatifida

^^^

Cut-leaf goodenia
Goodeniaceae
WA, NT, SA, Qld, NSW, Vic

This very pretty wildflower grows in inland shrublands and woodlands of semi-arid and arid regions. It has erect or spreading stems to 40 cm long and forms a basal rosette of narrow, oblong leaves, with several rather narrow lobes tapering into a long stalk. The stem leaves at the base of the branches are usually lobed while those on the floral stem are almost always entire. The numerous bright yellow flowers, often clustered, are borne at the ends of slender stems from late winter to early summer.

Hakea cinerea

^^^

Ashy hakea
Proteaceae
WA

An upright shrub to 3 m tall with felted branches and young growth. The stiff, grey-green, oblanceolate leaves to 13 cm long have conspicuous longitudinal veins and end with a small, sharp point. Bright yellow flowers are borne on the upper branches in axillary clusters mostly during spring. This species grows naturally in sand between Hopetoun and Esperance. In the garden provide a light, well-drained soil and a sunny position.

Helichrysum apiculatum

^^^

Common everlasting
Asteraceae
All States

This widespread species is extremely variable and a number of forms exist — from a prostrate carpeting plant with a suckering habit to an upright slender plant to 50 cm high. The stems are covered with white woolly hairs. Stem clasping linear leaves up to 7 cm long are also covered with a webbing of white hairs. Several flower heads are produced in clusters atop the stems. The small, individual, rounded flowers are bright yellow or golden with small, papery bracts. Many forms of this species are offered for sale. It likes lots of sun and good drainage.

Helichrysum bracteatum

^^^

Golden everlasting
Asteraceae
All States

Widespread over most of Australia this is an extremely variable species and many forms exist. In the centre the form likely to be found is an erect perennial to around 60 cm high with narrow oblanceolate, stem-clasping leaves to 10 cm long. The soft leaves are often woolly. The golden flower heads to 6 cm in diameter are surrounded by outer, shiny, yellow, papery bracts. A form found amongst granite rocks in south-west Western Australia grows to 1 m high and has red-brown bracts around the flower heads. This species and its many forms are widely known garden subjects.

Helichrysum eremaeum

^^^

ASTERACEAE

WA, SA, NT

This showy, dwarf perennial to around 50 cm high can be seen growing in sandy soils in the area around Ayers Rock, Northern Territory. It has a shrubby, rounded habit with many branches covered in white, woolly hairs. The linear leaves to 1.5 cm long are also covered in hairs. Small, button-like, bright yellow flowers to 1 cm across are held singly at the ends of stems, mostly during winter and spring.

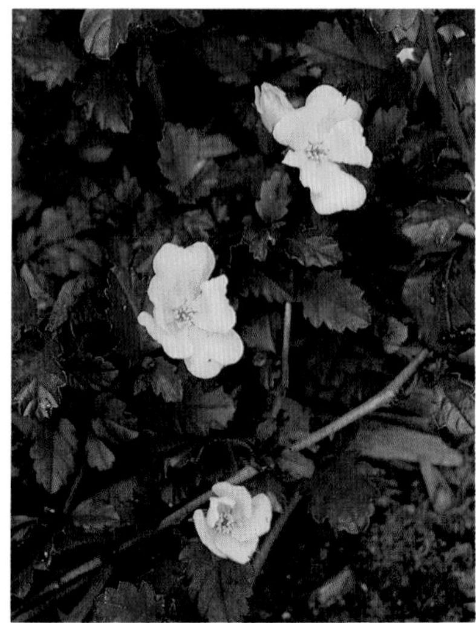

Hibbertia grossulariifolia

^^^

GOOSEBERRY-LEAVED GUINEA FLOWER

DILLENIACEAE

WA

This delightful prostrate plant forms a mat about 2 m across. It inhabits coastal heaths and forests of south-west Western Australia. Young reddish stems are softly hairy and dark green, oval leaves are coarsely toothed. Bright yellow flowers up to 1.5 m across are produced in late winter and spring.

Hibbertia hypericoides

^^^

YELLOW BUTTERCUP
DILLENIACEAE
WA

A small, spreading shrub found mostly in coastal areas and jarrah forests from Northampton to August. It is common in the woodlands of the Perth district. Narrow leaves to 1.5 cm long have a densely hairy undersurface. The deep yellow, buttercup-like flowers up to 2.5 cm across have deeply notched petals. These are produced mainly during winter and spring.

Hibbertia microphylla

^^^

DILLENIACEAE
WA

This small shrub to no more than 80 cm high occurs in the Albany district and the Stirling Range. It has minute, ovate leaves crowded along the stems and bears masses of small, yellow flowers from upper axils during the spring months. Its slight arching habit makes it a very attractive rockery and container plant. It requires adequate moisture and a light, well-drained soil.

Melaleuca globifera

^^^

MYRTACEAE
WA

An attractive tree to 10 m high with papery bark and broad, obovate leaves to 7 cm long with up to seven distinct nerves. The large, rounded, terminal, yellow flowers are produced during spring. It occurs in the Fitzgerald River National Park and the Recherche Archipelago.

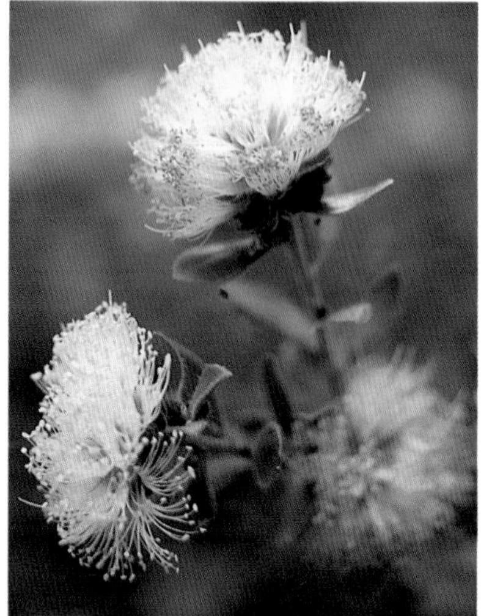

Melaleuca megacephala

^^^

MYRTACEAE
WA

This attractive flowering shrub inhabits sandy heaths in the Murchison River area. It is a dense, spreading shrub up to 3 m high with ovate leaves up to 2 cm long showing three prominent veins. The numerous pale yellow flowers with brown bracts are arranged in dense, terminal globular heads up to 3 cm across. These appear during spring to early summer.

Nuytsia floribunda

^^^

WESTERN AUSTRALIAN CHRISTMAS TREE
LORANTHACEAE
WA

This remarkable tree is closely related to the mistletoe and is parasitic on roots of other plants. It is common in the south-west of Western Australia, from the Murchison River to Israelite Bay on the south coast and is almost always found in sand. It grows up to 12 m high and has linear leaves. It bears masses of brilliant yellow to orange flowers in early summer.

Petrophile media

^^^

PROTEACEAE
WA

This small, rounded shrub to around 60 cm high occurs in the sandplains around Badgingarra and extends to the coast north of Perth. The terete leaves are stiff and pointed. Attractive velvety, creamy-yellow flowers are produced at branch ends during spring and early summer.

Petrophile serruriae

^^^

PROTEACEAE
WA

This attractive shrub with arching branches up to 2 m high grows on gravelly hillsides north of Perth. It has short, divided, rather stiff, prickly leaves and produces many small, soft, yellow flowers in the upper leaf axils and at the ends of drooping branches during spring.

Pittosporum phillyreoides

^^^

WEEPING PITTOSPORUM, BERRIGAN
PITTOSPORACEAE
ALL MAINLAND STATES

This small, slender tree to 4 m high is found in dry regions in a variety of woodland communities. It has rough, grey bark and pendulous branches with narrow, flat leaves to 10 cm long. Small, fragrant, pale yellow, tubular flowers with five spreading petals are followed by oval, fleshy fruit which ripens to bright orange. The leaves and wood from this plant were used medicinally by the Aborigines.

Senecio lautus

^^^

VARIABLE GROUNDSEL
ASTERACEAE
ALL STATES

This widespread and variable species occurs in a wide range of habitats. It grows on a variety of soils in Central Australia. It is a small annual or sometimes a perennial to 20 cm high with narrow or linear leaves which may be toothed or lobed. Showy, yellow, daisy-like flowers are borne in loose clusters at branch ends in late winter and early summer.

Synaphea petiolaris

^^^

PROTEACEAE
WA

This eye-catching small shrub, less than 1 m tall, can be seen growing in sand-heaths around Jurien, north of Perth. It has bright green leaves deeply divided into pungent points and attractive, elongated flower spikes composed of small, yellow, individual flowers up to 5 mm long. These appear in late winter and spring.

Verticordia chrysantha

^^^

GOLDEN FEATHER FLOWER

MYRTACEAE

WA

This upright, rounded shrub to 70 cm high is common over a wide area on the sandheaths. It has crowded, semi-terete leaves and numerous, large, yellow flowers in loose clusters throughout spring. This is an attractive species for the garden where it must have excellent drainage. In hot, exposed situations it appreciates some dappled shade.

Verticordia grandiflora

^^^

CLAW FEATHER FLOWER

MYRTACEAE

WA

This widespread species can be found from the Murchison River south to Ravensthorpe. It grows to around 1 m tall and has crowded linear leaves to 1.5 cm long. Masses of bright yellow flowers at branch ends are produced during spring. Flowers gradually change to a brownish-red as they age. This is a popular species in cultivation. It needs a sunny, open position in a well-drained soil.

Waitzia acuminata

^^^

ORANGE IMMORTELLE
ASTERACEAE
WA, NT, SA, NSW, VIC

This showy annual herb occurs in deep, sandy soils and red earths in drier regions of inland Australia. In some areas after good rain spectacular carpets of bright yellow flowers may be seen. It is a pubescent plant with linear leaves covered with short hairs. The elongated, golden-yellow, papery flowers are borne in clusters at the ends of upright stems. Packets of seeds of this lovely wildflower are fairly easy to buy. It is best sown in autumn and makes a delightful bedding and container plant.

Zygophyllum apiculatum

^^^

ZYGOPHYLLACEAE
ALL MAINLAND STATES

This low growing, shrub-like perennial occurs in arid regions in inland Australia. Each leaf is divided into two leaflets and many species in this genus are given the common name twin-leaf. This species has obovate leaflets to 4 cm long and bright yellow flowers consisting of five petals and ten stamens. The small, fleshy fruit has five wings.

Pink

F·L·O·W·E·R·S

Actinodium cunninghamii

^^^

Swamp daisy, Albany daisy
Myrtaceae
WA

This small, slender-branched shrub to less than 1 m tall has tiny narrow, aromatic, stem-clasping leaves. Daisy-like, flat-topped flowers to 4 cm across are creamy-white with pale pink centres. It flowers mostly in summer. It is found in moist localities from Albany east to Busselton.

Baeckea crassifolia

^^^

Desert Baeckea
Myrtaceae
WA, SA, NSW, Vic

This dwarf shrub is common in sandy heathlands in dry inland areas. It grows to around 50 cm high and has very small, rounded leaves. The flowers may be either white or various shades of pink and bloom through winter and spring. This pretty, but tough, small plant will withstand dry periods and is best suited to gardens in warm, low rainfall areas. Provide good drainage and a light, sandy soil.

Beaufortia schaueri

^^^

PINK BOTTLEBRUSH
MYRTACEAE
WA

A beautiful small shrub to 1 m tall found in sandy heaths and rocky hillsides from the Stirling Range eastwards to the Esperance area. It has small, narrow, pointed leaves and stiff, spreading branches. The pinky-mauve, rounded flower heads are carried on the ends of small branches throughout the spring months and at other times of the year. This species has adapted successfully to cultivation where it requires a dry, sunny position with very good drainage.

Boronia crenulata

^^^

RUTACEAE
WA

This upright dense shrub to 1 m high can be seen in mallee heath on the lower slopes of the Stirling Range. It has bright green, aromatic leaves to 1.5 cm long which are wedge-shaped with very small teeth. Masses of bright pink, star flowers in groups of up to three are borne in the upper axils and ends of branches during late winter and spring. This is a pretty boronia for a container or well-drained position in the garden. Keep watered in dry times and provide some light shade.

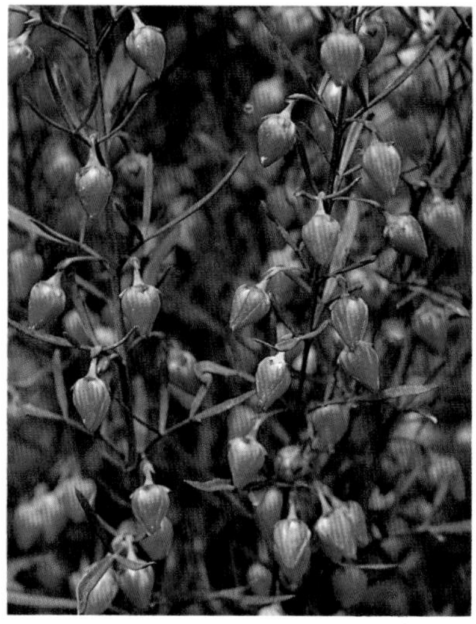

Boronia heterophylla

^^^

RED BORONIA, KALGAN BORONIA
RUTACEAE
WA

This beautiful rounded shrub to 2 m high occurs in the Kalgan and King River districts near Albany. The aromatic leaves may vary from narrow and simple to finely divided. The rose pink, pendulous, bell flowers have a light fragrance and bloom during spring. This species may be obtained from some nurseries specialising in native plants. Its roots must be kept cool and moist and it does best in part shade.

Boronia molloyae

^^^

TALL BORONIA
RUTACEAE
WA

An upright spreading shrub to 4 m. Branches and especially young stems are densely covered with tiny hairs. It can be seen in moist swampy sites in the Albany districts and west to Margaret River. The pendant, bright pink flowers are carried on numerous side branches during spring and summer. This species is best suited to a partly shaded position with plenty of water given in summer. A good mulch of compost or leaf mould will keep the roots cool and moist.

Boronia pulchella

^^^

RUTACEAE
WA

Found in the Stirling Ranges, this delightful small shrub to around 1 m high has a slight cascading habit. It has narrow, pinnate leaves which are aromatic when crushed and bears masses of bright pink, star flowers during spring. This species is uncommon in cultivation.

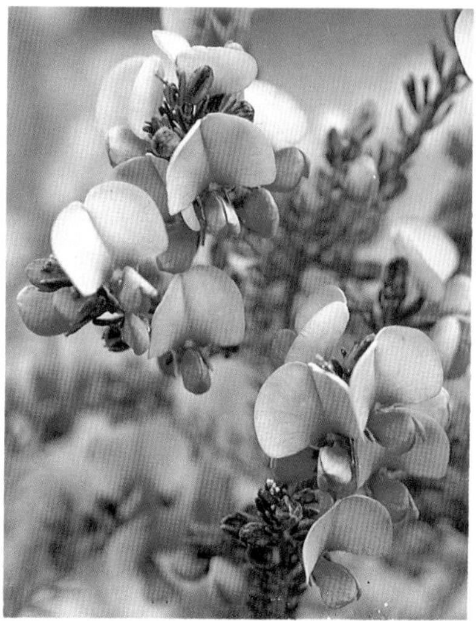

Burtonia scabra

^^^

PAINTED LADY
FABACEAE
WA

This outstanding, flowering, small shrub can be seen growing in sandy soils in the south-west of Western Australia. It grows to around 1 m tall with narrow leaves in groups of three. Masses of pinky-mauve, pea flowers are borne in the upper leaf axils during spring. A closely related species *B. villosa* differs in having a silky, hairy calyx. It is found only between Albany and the Stirling Range.

Caladenia reptans

^^^

Little pink fairy orchid
Orchidaceae
WA

This delightful, small, terrestrial orchid to no more than around 10 cm high is found in coastal heathlands as well as forested areas in south-west Western Australia. Its dainty, deep pink flowers are produced in late winter. Flowering is at its best in areas that have recently been burnt by a bushfire. *Caladenia* are among the more difficult terrestrial orchids to grow and are uncommon in cultivation.

Caladrinia remota

^^^

Round-leaved parakeelya
Portulaceae
WA, NT, SA

A low spreading plant with succulent cylindrical leaves. The shiny, pinky-mauve to purple flowers are borne on long, slender, ascending stems throughout the year and last for one day only. This species and the closely related *C. balonensis* occur on sandplains and dunes in dry inland areas.

Calytrix tetragona

^^^

FRINGE MYRTLE
MYRTACEAE
WA, SA, QLD, NSW, VIC, TAS

This attractive aromatic shrub has a wide distribution and varies from a dwarf to a medium shrub of around 2 m. The tiny, slender leaves to 6 mm long are crowded along the stem. Small, star-shaped flowers from white to shades of pink are borne in dense heads near branch ends in spring. After flowering the calyxes, which redden with age, remain on the plant for some weeks. This adaptable garden plant is best suited to a lightly shaded, well-drained position.

Chamelaucium ciliatum

^^^

MYRTACEAE
WA

This delightful small bushy shrub occurs in open sandplain heath country in south-west Western Australia. It grows up to 50 cm high with small, narrow leaves with a rounded tip. The crowded leaves are aromatic and have a fruity fragrance when crushed. Masses of small, white or pale pink flowers are borne in clusters towards the ends of the stems during spring. These age to a deep pink and finally to red giving the plant a most attractive appearance. This species is becoming popular in cultivation where it should be grown in an open position in well-drained, sandy soil.

Chamelaucium uncinatum

^^^

Geraldton wax
Myrtaceae
WA

This famous wildflower of the garden and florist both in Australia and overseas has its natural occurrence in sandplains north of Perth to around Kalbarri. It grows to around 2 m or more high with many spreading branches and small, linear leaves with a hooked tip. Try crushing and smelling a leaf. It is reminiscent of 'Juicy Fruit' chewing gum. The clusters of large, waxy flowers can be seen in white or pink to purply-red with a dark red centre. These appear from late winter and during spring. In the garden provide good drainage. Pruning after flowering will improve shape and vigour.

Dryandra carlinoides

^^^

Proteaceae
WA

This is an attractive, low growing, upright shrub to about 1 m with lanceolate leaves to 3 cm long. The leaves are slightly rolled under and have a few scattered teeth ending in a sharp point. It occurs in sandplains and heaths between Perth and Kalbarri. Abundant pinkish-cream flowers borne at the ends of almost all the branches in spring make this a spectacular sight. It is uncommon in cultivation.

Eremophila calorhabdos

^^^

RED ROD, SPIKED EREMOPHILA
MYOPORACEAE
WA

An attractive upright shrub usually found on sandy soils in woodlands of semi-arid regions in southern Western Australia. It grows to around 2 m tall and has crowded, ovate to lanceolate leaves to 2.5 cm with fine serrations towards the tip. The tubular, pinky-red flowers have curled back lobed tips and extended stamens. These are borne in the axils of the upper leaves during spring and summer. This species is successful in cultivation and is best suited to a sunny, well-drained position.

Eremophila pachyphylla

^^^

MYOPORACEAE
WA

A neat, upright shrub to 3 m high found in eucalypt woodlands in semi-arid regions in southern Western Australia. It has smooth, elliptic-lanceolate leaves to 2.5 cm long with a hooked, pointed tip. The very pale mauve-pink, tubular flowers have a darker mauve calyx. Flowers are often profuse and are produced singly or in threes along the branches mostly during spring.

Eriostemon spicatus

^^^

SPIKED WAX FLOWER, PEPPER AND SALT
RUTACEAE
WA

A very pretty aromatic plant to 1 m high found in sandy soils of the coastal plain from the Geraldton area south to Albany. It has narrow glandular leaves to 2 cm long and pinkish-mauve star flowers during winter and spring. Grow in an open sunny position in the garden with very good drainage.

Geranium solanderi

^^^

AUSTRAL CRANE'S BILL
GERANIACEAE
WA, SA, QLD, NSW, VIC, TAS

This low growing, prostrate perennial with a spread of up to 1.5 m is covered with soft hairs. It is widely distributed and is found mainly in dry districts of temperate Australia. The deeply dissected, light green leaves have up to seven lobes. Pale pink, five petalled flowers are borne in pairs at the end of a stem up to 4 cm long mainly during spring and summer.

Gossypium sturtianum

^^^

STURT'S DESERT ROSE
MALVACEAE
WA, NT, SA, QLD, NSW, VIC

This beautiful desert plant found over much of the dry interior, is the floral emblem of the Northern Territory. Good examples can be seen on the way to Standley Chasm after Jay Creek, Northern Territory. It is an erect slender shrub to 2 m tall with green or grey-green, ovate to rounded leaves. The green stems, calyx and fruit are marked with black glandular spots. The showy hibiscus-like flowers are pink, lilac or white with a reddish blotch at the throat. Flowers are produced almost continuously throughout the year, especially after good rain. This is an attractive plant for inland gardens. Provide good drainage.

Grevillea petrophiloides

^^^

PINK POKERS, POKER GREVILLEA
PROTEACEAE
WA

This beautiful grevillea can be seen growing in sandy and gravelly soils in tall scrub in the northern wheatbelt region of Western Australia. It grows up to 1 m or more high and has divided, grey-green leaves with very narrow segments ending with a sharp point. The pink, cylindrical flowers up to 8 cm long are produced during winter and early spring. In the garden this species is best suited to a dry climate and very well-drained soil.

Grevillea quercifolia

^^^

OAK-LEAF GREVILLEA
PROTEACEAE
WA

An interesting understorey shrub from the jarrah forests of Western Australia. It grows to around 1 m high and has dark-green, prickly, lobed leaves. The pinky-purple flowers are borne on erect terminal spikes during spring. This species is best suited to a partially shaded, well-drained position in the garden. It can be found in some specialist nurseries.

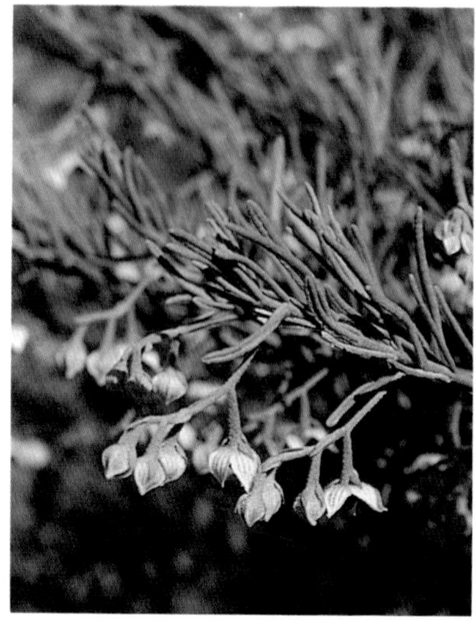

Guichenotia ledifolia

^^^

STERCULIACEAE
WA

A small, branched shrub to 1 m with a felted covering found over a wide area in the south-west of Western Australia. The grey-green, narrow leaves up to 5 cm long have rolled under margins. Pale, dusty-pink, pendulous flowers are borne in loose sprays during late winter and spring. This and the following species of *Guichenotia* can be found in some native plant nurseries. Grow in a partially shaded, well-drained position. Prune after flowering to maintain compact shape.

Guichenotia macrantha

^^^

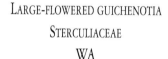

LARGE-FLOWERED GUICHENOTIA
STERCULIACEAE
WA

This species can be seen on sandy or gravelly soils in drier areas of the south-west of Western Australia. It is a dense, rounded shrub to 1 m and has narrow, grey-green leaves to 7 cm long. The showy, pinky-purple, bell-shaped flowers in groups of up to three are produced in winter and spring. This is an attractive small plant for the garden or rockery pocket and may be grown in coastal areas with some protection.

Guichenotia micrantha

^^^

SMALL-FLOWERED GUICHENOTIA
STERCULIACEAE
WA

This is a very pretty small shrub when in flower. It is found in coastal areas of the south-west of Western Australia and further inland to semi-arid and arid districts. It grows up to 1.5 m high with a dense, downy covering and has small linear leaves to 3 cm long. The dainty, pinkish-purple flowers which hang in small arching sprays are abundant and showy during winter and spring.

Hakea cucullata

^^^

Scallops, Cup hakea
Proteaceae
WA

This erect shrub varying from 2 to 5 m high is common in the Stirling Range and Albany districts. The attractive, cup-shaped leaves with crinkled edges support clusters of deep pink flowers. These are produced in profusion mostly during winter and early spring. This bird-attracting, decorative plant does well in temperate regions in a very well-drained, light soil.

Hakea multilineata

^^^

Grass-leaved hakea
Proteaceae
WA

This tall erect shrub to 5 m high occurs on gravelly heaths in the southern wheatbelt region of Western Australia. It has broad-linear flat leaves to 18 cm long with up to fifteen longitudinal veins ending with a rounded tip. The bright pink flowers are produced in elongated spikes up to 4 cm long mostly during spring. This species is often confused with *H. francisiana* but is characterised by its shorter congested racemes. In the garden provide good drainage and a sunny position.

Hakea petiolaris

^^^

SEA URCHIN HAKEA
PROTEACEAE
WA

An upright shrub or small tree to 10 m tall found in the vicinity of granite rocks in the southern wheatbelt region. It has rigid, wiry branches and grey-green, ovate leaves to 15 cm long. The pinkish pincushion-type flowers with cream-coloured stamens are produced on the older wood during winter. This popular species in cultivation is well suited to semi-arid and warm temperate areas. It will grow in most well-drained soils in a sunny position.

Helipterum roseum

^^^

PINK PAPER-DAISY
ASTERACEAE
WA

This delightful annual plant occurs in sandy soils over a wide area of south-west Western Australia, usually slightly inland. It is an erect, clumping plant to around 40 cm high with grey-green stems and narrow leaves. The white, pale pink or deep pink flowers are produced singly at the ends of the stems mostly during winter and spring. This popular bedding plant can be grown from seed sown directly into the soil. It needs good drainage and plenty of sun.

Hemiandra pungens

^^^

SNAKEBUSH
LAMIACEAE
WA

This small spreading shrub is found on the coastal sandplains from Dongara to Albany and in the heathlands of the jarrah forests. It has rigid pointed leaves and masses of pinky-mauve flowers with pink spotted throats in spring and summer. The prostrate form of this plant is popular as a rockery subject. It likes a light, well-drained soil and plenty of sun.

Hypocalymma angustifolium

^^^

WHITE MYRTLE
MYRTACEAE
WA

This small, bushy shrub to around 1 m high is found mostly in coastal areas from Northampton to Albany, but can also be seen some distance inland. It has very narrow, aromatic leaves to 4 cm long ending with a point. The white flowers are often pink at the throat and deepen to a dark pink with age. This is a pretty, small shrub for the garden where it prefers a sheltered position with a little shade and a cool root run.

Hypocalymma robustum

^^^

Swan River myrtle
Myrtaceae
WA

This lovely wildflower of the coastal plains and jarrah forests between Perth and Albany has a beautiful fragrance. It is a small, erect shrub to around 1 m high with stiff, linear leaves to 3 cm long. Masses of pink double flowers are clustered along the branches during winter and early spring. In cultivation this species appreciates a light, well-drained soil and a good mulch to help keep the root area cool.

Indigofera leucotricha

^^^

Silver indigo
Fabaceae
WA, NT, SA, NSW

This small shrub to 1 m high is found mostly on inland slopes and ridges. It is covered with dense, woolly hairs and has attractive grey-green, pinnate leaves composed of up to seventeen leaflets. Showy, deep pink, pea-shaped flowers are borne on erect sprays up to 6 cm long.

Isopogon cuneatus

^^^

Proteaceae
WA

An erect, many-branched shrub to 2 m found on heaths and woodlands in the lower south-west of Western Australia. It has obovate leaves to 10 cm long with a rounded tip and large, terminal, rose-pink flower heads up to 5 cm across. *Isopogon latifolius* is similar, but is confined to the Stirling Range, has larger flower heads up to 8 cm across and the leaves end in a sharp point.

Isopogon divergens

^^^

Spreading coneflower
Proteaceae
WA

This highly ornamental shrub is found on open heaths and woodlands in granite or gravelly soil mostly from Perth to the Murchison River district. It is a spreading, small shrub to 1.5 m tall with terete, sharply pointed, divided leaves. In late winter and spring it is covered with many pinky-mauve, silky flowers up to 5 cm across.

Isopogon dubius

^^^

PINCUSHION CONEFLOWER
PROTEACEAE
WA

An attractive, small shrub to 1.5 m high frequently seen in the jarrah forests north and east of Perth. It has prickly, flat, deeply segmented leaves and masses of terminal heads of rose-pink flowers measuring up to 5 cm across. This species is well known in cultivation and will grow in the eastern states. It needs good drainage, plenty of sun and will tolerate dry periods.

Isopogon formosus

^^^

ROSE CONEFLOWER
PROTEACEAE
WA

This eye-catching rounded shrub to 1.5 m tall is common in the south-west of Western Australia and is frequently seen in the woodlands north of Albany and the Stirling Range. Its leaves are deeply divided into pointed, terete segments which separate it from the similar *I. dubius* which has flat leaf segments. Large, terminal, pink flowers to 6 cm across are produced in late winter and early spring. This lovely species resents summer humidity and is only successful in temperate regions with winter rainfall. It requires excellent drainage in a lightly textured soil.

Kunzea affinis

^^^

MYRTACEAE

WA

This lovely many-branched shrub to 1.5 m tall occurs in sandy soils in southern Western Australia from the Stirling Range to Israelite Bay. It has narrow leaves up to 6 mm long and bears masses of rose-pink flowers in small clusters at the ends of the stems during spring. This species is successful in cultivation and is best suited to a light, well-drained soil. Tip prune from early days to encourage compact shape.

Kunzea jucunda

^^^

MYRTACEAE

WA

This highly floriferous shrub is found in the lower south-west of Western Australia. It is an open shrub to 2 m tall with minute obovate, bright green leaves. Masses of fluffy rose-pink flowers are produced in small clusters at the ends of branchlets from late winter to mid spring.

Kunzea preissiana

^^^

MYRTACEAE

WA

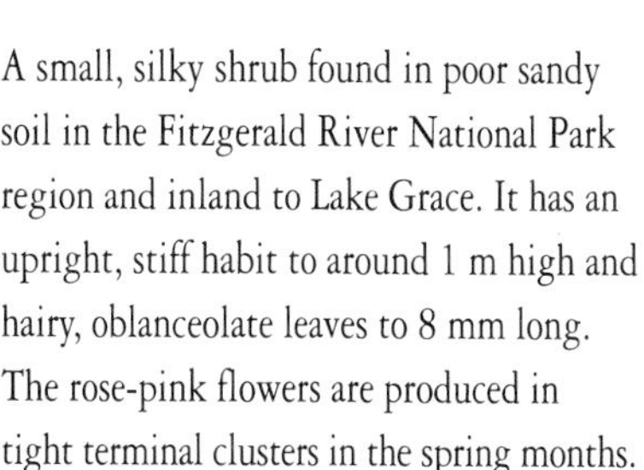

A small, silky shrub found in poor sandy soil in the Fitzgerald River National Park region and inland to Lake Grace. It has an upright, stiff habit to around 1 m high and hairy, oblanceolate leaves to 8 mm long. The rose-pink flowers are produced in tight terminal clusters in the spring months.

Leptospermum sericeum

^^^

SILVER TEA-TREE

MYRTACEAE

WA

This very pretty, silky shrub to 2 m tall is found around Cape Le Grande and the Recherche Archipelago. It has a spreading habit and obovate, soft, silky leaves. The large flowers up to 2.5 cm across open white and age to deep pink mostly during spring and again in late summer. This species is popular in cultivation where it is best suited to a sunny, well-drained position.

Melaleuca filifolia

(Syn. *M. nematophylla*)

^^^

WIRY HONEY MYRTLE

MYRTACEAE

WA

This very beautiful plant is found on the sandplains and heaths north of Perth. It forms an erect shrub to 2 m high and has alternate, linear or terete leaves to 10 cm long. The pinky-purple flowers are arranged in rounded terminal heads. Flowers appear from late winter to mid spring. In the garden it requires an open, sunny, well-drained position.

Melaleuca nesophila

^^^

SHOWY HONEY MYRTLE

MYRTACEAE

WA

This attractive species occurs on coastal sandy heaths of southern Western Australia. It forms a dense shrub to around 2.5 m high with slender branches bearing alternate, ovate leaves to 2 cm long. The pink or mauve flowers are arranged in rounded terminal heads, the axis having continuous growth after flowering. Flowers can be seen during spring and summer. This very popular plant in cultivation is hardy in most soils or situations but prefers an open position with good drainage.

Melaleuca pulchella

^^^

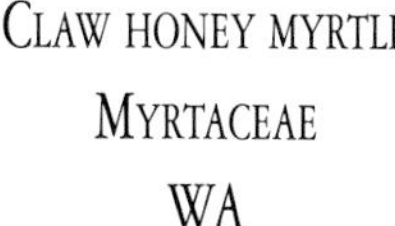

CLAW HONEY MYRTLE
MYRTACEAE
WA

This small, spreading shrub to around 1 m high occurs on southern coastal heaths between Hopetoun and Israelite Bay. It has small, crowded, ovate leaves with prominent oil glands on the undersurface. The purplish-pink flowers may be solitary or with up to three together along the branches. The flowers are composed of five, claw-like segments enclosing numerous short stamens. They appear during spring and summer. An attractive and adaptable species for the garden that benefits from pruning immediately after flowering.

Melaleuca radula

^^^

GRACEFUL HONEY MYRTLE
MYRTACEAE
WA

An upright spreading shrub that inhabits drier inland granite outcrops. It grows to about 1.5 m high with slender branches and opposite linear leaves to 4 cm long. The pink or mauve flowers tipped with golden anthers are in fairly dense spikes during spring and summer. In cultivation this adaptable species prefers a warm climate and will withstand periods of dryness. It is best suited to a well-drained, sunny position.

Melaleuca scabra

^^^

ROUGH HONEY MYRTLE

MYRTACEAE

WA

This magnificent flowering bush has a wide distribution over much of south-west Western Australia. It grows to around 2 m high. The very slender, terete leaves to 2.5 cm long may be smooth, crinkled or warty. The deep pink or magenta flowers with golden anthers appear in dense terminal heads in great numbers, almost covering the bush. They can be seen throughout spring to around mid summer. This beautiful small plant for the warm temperate garden will grow in most well-drained soils.

Melaleuca spathulata

^^^

MYRTACEAE

WA

This outstanding plant of sandy coastal plains of southern Western Australia is also found in the Stirling Range. It is a small, spreading shrub with slender branches to around 1.5 m high. New growth is silky-pubescent. The tiny, scattered, obovate leaves may be spreading or recurved. Terminal heads of rounded, pinkish-mauve flowers appear in profusion in late spring and summer. A very pretty plant for the garden, best suited to good drainage and full sun. Prune immediately after flowering to encourage leafy growth and good flower production.

Melaleuca spicigera

^^^

MYRTACEAE
WA

This small, branching shrub is found in sandy heaths and granite rocky areas in south-west Western Australia. It grows to around 1.5 m high, often with arching branches and has ovate, glandular leaves that are stem-clasping and frequently pointed downwards. The pinkish-mauve, pompom flowers are borne on short stems on the previous year's growth. This species is very attractive in flower which is most often during the second half of spring. In cultivation it prefers full sun and is moderately frost resistant.

Melaleuca suberosa

^^^

CORKY HONEY MYRTLE
MYRTACEAE
WA

This unusual small shrub to no more than 1 m high occurs on southern sandheaths from Albany to Israelite Bay. It has tiny, crowded, linear leaves with a warty appearance. From the corky bark, masses of pinky-purple flowers emerge forming long clusters along the branches. Flowers are at their best in early spring.

Petrophile linearis

^^^

PIXIE MOPS
PROTEACEAE
WA

This small but beautiful shrub inhabits sandy coastal areas from south of Perth to Jurien. It grows to less than 1 m in height and has thick, sickle-shaped leaves to 8 cm long. The soft, woolly, pink flower heads to 5 cm across are produced at branch ends during spring.

Pimelea ferruginea

^^^

PINK RICE FLOWER
THYMELAEACEAE
WA

This neat, free flowering shrub has for many years been in cultivation. It occurs naturally on coastal dunes in the south-west of Western Australia and may be grown in a protected seaside garden. Provide good drainage and lots of sun. It grows to 1 m high and broad and has oval, glossy leaves in two pairs of uniform rows. In spring the whole of the bush is covered in bright pink, pincushion flowers.

Pimelea rosea

^^^

ROSE BANJINE
THYMELAEACEAE
WA

A slender, erect shrub to 1 m that is common on the Swan Coastal Plain. The leaves are linear-lanceolate to 2 cm long and hooked at the ends. The silky, pink flowers to 3 cm diameter are produced in late winter and spring. This is a pretty plant for the garden. Grow in a light, well-drained soil in full sun or dappled shade. Prune immediately after flowering to promote bushy growth.

Pterocaulon sphacelatum

^^^

FRUIT SALAD PLANT, APPLE BUSH
ASTERACEAE
WA, NT, SA, QLD, NSW

This erect, small plant to 60 cm high is covered with brownish hairs. It is common in inland areas and occurs in low lying areas on flood and gibber plains. The narrow oblong leaves to 5 cm long are soft and wrinkled. When crushed they emit a fruity odour which gives rise to this plant's common names. The pinkish, globular flower heads are produced at the ends of stems mostly in spring.

Ptilotus obovatus

^^^

SILVERY TAILS
AMARANTHACEAE
ALL MAINLAND STATES

This variable, shrubby plant to 1 m tall is covered in silvery-grey hairs giving it a whitish appearance. It is widely distributed in the drier regions of Australia and is the most common species of *Ptilotus*. It has greyish-white, obovate leaves and pale pink oval flowers to 1.5 cm wide which are covered in white hairs. They are produced singly or in groups at the ends of the branchlets for most of the year. This is a most attractive silver plant for the semi-arid garden or rockery. Provide a light, well-drained soil and plenty of sun.

Scholtzia laxiflora

^^^

SCHOLTZIA
MYRTACEAE
WA

This lovely flowering plant is found on the sandplains and heath north of Perth. It is a tall slender shrub to 2 m with minute, obovate leaves and masses of small, pink, tea-tree-like flowers produced in loose clusters near the ends of the branchlets in late winter and spring.

Thomasia macrocarpa

^^^

LARGE FRUITED THOMASIA
STERCULIACEAE
WA

A most attractive, spreading shrub to around 1 m high with crinkled short-lobed leaves which may be very pubescent when young. Masses of pale pink or mauve pendant flowers with a papery appearance are produced at branch ends in late winter and spring. This popular species in cultivation enjoys a light, well-drained soil in full sun or dappled shade.

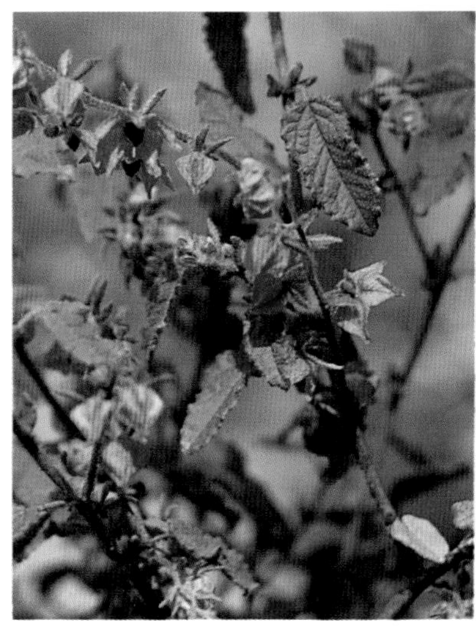

Thomasia petalocalyx

^^^

PAPER FLOWER
STERCULIACEAE
WA

This spreading shrub to 1 m high is found in southern coastal areas of Western Australia. The soft, oblong leaves to 5 cm long have undulate margins. Pendant, pinkish-mauve, papery flowers are produced in loose clusters from late winter through to spring. This is an ideal, salt-tolerant, small shrub for seaside gardens.

Thomasia pygmaea

^^^

TINY THOMASIA
STERCULIACEAE
WA

This delightful, small shrub to 60 cm tall occurs in southern parts of Western Australia. It has small, rounded, heart-shaped leaves. The masses of dainty, pendulous flowers which are pinky-mauve with small red dots almost cover the plant in full flower during late winter and spring. This very pretty plant can be obtained from nurseries specialising in native plants. Provide good drainage and cut back after flowering to encourage compact shape.

Thryptomene maisonneuvii

^^^

MYRTACEAE
WA, NT, SA

This low spreading shrub to 1.5 m is found in arid regions on red sand and can be seen growing around Uluru (Ayers Rock) and on the road to Alice Springs, Northern Territory. It has minute leaves crowded along the slender branches. Small, pinky-white flowers with five rounded petals are produced generously in winter and spring.

Verticordia lindleyi

^^^

MYRTACEAE

WA

A small, dainty shrub to no more than 60 cm high found on sandy heaths from around Eneabba to just south of Perth. It has slender stems and small, spreading, oval leaves with conspicuous oil dots. The pale pink flowers have a feathery calyx and pretty fringed or toothed petals. These appear mostly in late spring and summer.

Verticordia picta

^^^

PAINTED FEATHER FLOWER

MYRTACEAE

WA

This small shrub up to 1 m tall is common on the sandheaths of south-west Western Australia. It has small pairs of linear leaves less than 1 cm long. Masses of deep pink flowers are produced during late winter and spring. Unlike most other species, the rounded pink petals are more conspicuous than the fringed calyx lobes below them. This species does well in cultivation. It requires excellent drainage and a light soil.

^^^ *Orange and Red* ^^^

F·L·O·W·E·R·S

Adenanthos obovata

^^^

BASKET FLOWER

PROTEACEAE

WA

Most of the 33 species of *Adenanthos* are found in the south-west of Western Australia. This eye-catching species occurs in sandy and swampy places and is common between Albany to just north of Perth. It is a small, many-stemmed shrub up to 1 m high with ovate leaves to 2 cm that are broadest towards the tip. The bright scarlet, tubular flowers have long styles which protrude well beyond the tube. These are produced throughout the winter months. This plant is regularly visited by nectar-eating birds and does well in a light, porous soil with good drainage.

Allocasuarina humilis

^^^

SCRUB SHE-OAK

CASUARINACEAE

WA

This small shrub to less than 2 m high has a wide distribution in the south-west of Western Australia and occurs mostly on sandy soils. This is a monoecious species which means it bears male and female flowers on the same plant. The male flowers are like tiny, cylindrical spikes borne on branch ends while the female flowers are like small, red tassels produced on the older wood. The latter form next season's cone-like fruits.

Anigozanthos manglesii

^^^

RED AND GREEN KANGAROO PAW
HAEMODORACEAE
WA

This best known and well-loved kangaroo paw is the floral emblem of Western Australia. It is a common natural plant in Kings Park in Perth and occurs on the sandplains from Shark Bay south to the Busselton area. It is a tufted perennial with grey-green, linear leaves to 60 cm long. The velvety flower stem and base are bright scarlet but change for the rest of the flower to a brilliant green. In populations south of Perth the flowers are borne mainly on single stems while northern populations have branched flower stems. Flowers appear during winter and spring.

Anigozanthos rufus

^^^

RED KANGAROO PAW
HAEMODORACEAE
WA

This species has branched, flowering stems up to 1.5 m high carrying striking, red flowers clothed with purple or burgundy hairs. Flowers appear mostly in spring and summer. It occurs in sandy areas mainly near the coast and is common between Esperance and Ravensthorpe. In cultivation this is an extremely ornamental species. It requires light, well-drained soils and plenty of sun.

Banksia ashbyi

^^^

ASHBY'S BANKSIA
PROTEACEAE
WA

A medium to large shrub with long narrow leaves up to 50 cm long which are deeply lobed almost to the mid-rib. It occurs in red, sandy country from just south of Geraldton to Carnarvon to the North West Cape where it is fairly common on coastal dunes. The rich orange, upright flower spikes appear mostly during the winter months. This is a spectacular banksia for warm, well-drained positions in the garden.

Banksia baueri

^^^

POSSUM BANKSIA
PROTEACEAE
WA

This distinctive species is easily identified by the large, soft flower spikes ranging in colour from a grey-mauve to a bright rusty-tan colour seen in some populations east of Ravensthorpe and on the Barren Ranges. The flowers are often produced near to the ground or within the bush and may be overlooked. It grows to a small to medium-sized shrub and is reasonably easy to grow if given a light, well-drained soil.

Banksia blechnifolia

^^^

PROTEACEAE
WA

This prostrate banksia can be seen growing in white sand in low heath between Jerramungup and just north of Esperance in the south-west of Western Australia. Its stems grow along the ground and often become covered with sand. It has erect, deeply-lobed, blue-green leaves up to 45 cm long. New growth is densely hairy. The flowers are a rusty-red becoming cream towards the base. They appear from September to November.

Banksia coccinea

^^^

SCARLET BANKSIA, ALBANY BANKSIA
PROTEACEAE
WA

This erect, slender-branched shrub produces beautiful, bright scarlet and grey flower heads set in a rosette of leaves from winter to mid summer. It is common on the coastal shrubland between Albany and east of Hopetoun and also occurs in low open woodland in the Stirling Range. In the garden this species likes the conditions of its home state preferring a dry summer, a light porous soil and excellent drainage.

Banksia menziesii

^^^

MENZIES BANKSIA
PROTEACEAE
WA

This is a beautiful banksia in flower, foliage and charming gnarled form. It is common on coastal plains from just north of Perth to the Shark Bay area. It grows to 10 m or more high with spreading branches and wavy, grey-green, toothed leaves. The lovely acorn-shaped, reddish-pink flowers are produced mostly in autumn and winter. This species is grown commercially for the cut-flower trade and this is the best time to buy from the flower markets.

Banksia occidentalis

^^^

RED SWAMP BANKSIA
PROTEACEAE
WA

This erect shrub to 4 m or more high, grows in swampy, peaty sands along the south coast from Augusta to Cape Arid. It has whorled and sparsely toothed, linear leaves with a whitish undersurface. The attractive crimson flower spikes are produced in great numbers mostly in summer and autumn, but some flowers can be seen at other times. This species adapts well to garden conditions provided it is well watered during dry times.

Beaufortia decussata

^^^

GRAVEL BOTTLEBRUSH
MYRTACEAE
WA

This upright shrub to around 2 m high can be seen in jarrah forests near Albany and in the Stirling Range. The oval leaves are arranged in opposite rows up the stem and rich red, oblong flower spikes are composed of long-clawed stamens arranged in bundles. These are produced mostly during summer. Some species of *Beaufortia* are available at specialised native plant nurseries and must be planted in a well-drained position. A light pruning in spring, before new growth begins, will help promote compact plants.

Beaufortia heterophylla

^^^

STIRLING RANGE BOTTLEBRUSH
MYRTACEAE
WA

This attractive small shrub to 1.5 m is found mostly in the Stirling Range. The narrow, grey-green leaves to 1 cm long are often scattered with fine hairs. In spring the plant is massed with deep red tufts of flowers. This species is uncommon in cultivation.

Beaufortia sparsa

^^^

SWAMP BOTTLEBRUSH
MYRTACEAE
WA

This spectacular flowering shrub inhabits swampy soils in the Albany district. It forms an open shrub to 3 m high with ovate, stem-clasping leaves arranged in pairs in opposite rows along the branches. The reddish-orange flower spikes to 7 cm across consist of many stamens bundled around the stem. Flowers are produced mainly in late summer and early autumn. This species sometimes can be obtained from specialist nurseries. In the garden it requires good drainage, but needs plenty of water during dry weather.

Beaufortia squarrosa

^^^

SAND BOTTLEBRUSH
MYRTACEAE
WA

This colourful wildflower can be seen growing on coastal plains and sandy heaths on the west coast of Western Australia north to the Murchison River. It is an upright, open shrub to around 1 m high with stem-clasping reflexed leaves less than 5 mm long. The terminal crimson flowers are in open heads up to 3 cm across. These are very numerous during spring and summer with a few flowers on the bush at other times of the year.

Billardiera erubescens

^^^

RED BILLARDIERA
PITTOSPORACEAE
WA

This attractive slender climber has dark green, oval-lanceolate leaves up to 7 cm long. Bright red, tubular flowers in loose clusters of up to eight flowers are produced throughout spring and summer. It occurs in sandheaths in the south-west of Western Australia and can often be seen scrambling to a height of 4.5 m over shrubs and low growing trees. This species can be obtained from native plant nurseries. It does best in a sunny, well-drained position.

Blancoa canescens

^^^

RED BUGLE, WINTER BELL
HAEMODORACEAE
WA

It is always a delight to come across this lovely wildflower, common on sandplains in the Hill River district, north of Perth. It is a small perennial herb to 30 cm high. The flat, grey, pubescent leaves to 25 cm long narrow to a soft point. Pendulous, felted, tubular flowers to 4 cm long are red on the outside and golden-orange within. They are produced throughout winter.

Brachysema celsianum

(Syn. *B. lanceolatum*)

^^^

SWAN RIVER PEA BUSH

FABACEAE

WA

This spreading small shrub or semi-climber to 1.5 m high and across has velvety branches with silver hairs. The olive-green, lanceolate leaves to 10 cm long also have a silvery undersurface. The striking red, pea flowers with a silvery calyx are borne singly or in small clusters along the stem mostly during winter to mid spring. This species is a popular bird-attracting plant and has adapted well to a wide range of soils and climatic conditions. It does well in full sun or light shade.

Brachysema praemorsum

^^^

FABACEAE

WA

A trailing, groundcovering plant with a spread of up to 1.5 m. It has decorative, dark green, fan-shaped leaves with a cut-off tip. The pea-shaped flowers are initially cream, then age to dark red. They are produced in opposite pairs mostly in autumn and winter. This species has adapted well to cultivation where it is used to trail over banks, rockeries and large containers. It does best in light shade.

Brachysema subcordatum

^^^

FABACEAE

WA

A small, rounded shrub to 1.5 m with silky new growth. The wavy-edged, rounded leaves are opposite or in whorls. The small flowers to 1 cm long are dark red. They are produced in late winter and spring. This species is uncommon in cultivation.

Callistemon glaucus

(Syn. *C. speciosus*)

^^^

ALBANY BOTTLEBRUSH

MYRTACEAE

WA

This upright stiff shrub to 3 m occurs on the margins of wet swamps of the Albany district. The narrow, leathery leaves with a prominent mid-rib are up to 15 cm long. Large, deep red flowers are produced in spring and summer. This outstanding species has been in cultivation for many years. It is especially suited to wet, problem areas in full sun. Prune when young and after flowering to encourage compact growth.

Calothamnus quadrifidus

^^^

COMMON NET-BUSH
MYRTACEAE
WA

This species occurs over a wide range of soils throughout the south-west of Western Australia. It is an upright dense shrub to 3 m. The pine-like leaves up to 3 cm long are sometimes sharply pointed and may be covered in fine hairs. The prominent flowers composed of bundles of four rich red stamens are borne in one-sided spikes in spring and summer. This is the most popular species of the genus in cultivation and once established will thrive in a wide range of soils and climatic conditions. Prune lightly after flowering to encourage shapely growth.

Calothamnus rupestris

^^^

CLIFF NET-BUSH
MYRTACEAE
WA

A large, spreading shrub to 2 m with thick, crooked branches often growing on granite outcrops of the Darling Range east of Perth. It has needle-like leaves to about 5 cm long and bears pinkish-red flowers in four bundles of stamens. These are in one-sided spikes and are produced mainly in spring. An attractive ornamental shrub for a well-drained open position.

Calothamnus validus

^^^

BARRENS CLAW-FLOWER
MYRTACEAE
WA

A small upright shrub that occurs in rocky hills of the Barren Ranges. The terete leaves to 3 cm long are slightly curved. Bundles of bright red, claw-flowers up to 4 cm long are produced in spring and summer. This species contributes greatly to the beautiful endemic flora of the Fitzgerald River National Park. It is uncommon in cultivation.

Chorilaena quercifolia

^^^

CHORILAENA
RUTACEAE
WA

This attractive, felted plant can be seen as an undershrub in the karri forests. It grows to around 3 m tall and has lobed, oak-shaped leaves with a densely hairy under-surface. The pendant flower heads, surrounded by linear bracts, may be cream, green or red. Flowers appear during spring to early summer. It is not often seen in cultivation.

Chorizema cordatum

^^^

HEART-LEAVED FLAME PEA
FABACEAE
WA

This colourful understorey shrub of the forests of south-west Western Australia has become a very popular garden shrub. It grows to around 2 m high with long, slender branches with a light twining habit. The heart-shaped leaves up to 5 cm long can be toothed or lobed. Masses of orange-red or yellow, pea-shaped flowers with a pink keel are produced from late winter to early summer. Plants are available from many nurseries which sell native plants. It is best planted with some shade in a moist, but well-drained position.

Chorizema dicksonii

^^^

YELLOW-EYED FLAME PEA
FABACEAE
WA

A small undershrub of the jarrah forests with numerous short open branches to around 1 m high. The slightly ovate, dark green leaves to around 2 cm long end with a sharp point. Bright orange-red, pea-shaped flowers with a yellow blotch at the throat are carried in terminal racemes during spring. This species is also well known in cultivation where it prefers part shade in a well-drained position.

Clianthus formosus

^^^

STURT'S DESERT PEA

FABACEAE

WA, NT, SA, QLD, NSW

This wonderful wildflower of Australia's inland is the floral emblem of South Australia. It is a softly-hairy annual or perennial plant which covers large areas after good rains, putting on an unforgettable display when in flower. The pinnate, grey-green leaves are covered with silky hairs and five or six large, scarlet, pea-shaped flowers to 9 cm long are held in erect back-to-back clusters. Flowers usually have a shiny black boss on the standard, but there are some which are completely scarlet and there is a rare red-and-white flower. Seeds are best sown in the position where the plant is to grow.

Darwinia citriodora

^^^

LEMON-SCENTED MYRTLE

MYRTACEAE

WA

This popular garden shrub has its natural home in the jarrah forests of the south-west of Western Australia. It grows to around 2 m tall and has neat, opposite, ovate leaves that when crushed are aromatic, but are not obviously lemon-scented as the specific name implies. The flower heads are composed of four to six reddish flowers with prominent styles. These are surrounded by red and green outer bracts. Flowers appear through winter and spring. In the garden it prefers a moist but well-drained soil and a little shade.

Darwinia lejostyla

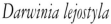

^^^

Myrtaceae
WA

This striking, small, heath-like shrub is widespread in the Stirling Ranges. It grows to 1 m high and has crowded, aromatic leaves to 1 cm long. The deep pink or red, pendant, bell-shaped flowers are surrounded by green outer bracts. Flowers are produced in spring. This highly ornamental plant can be obtained from some nurseries specialising in the sale of native plants. It does best in an open sunny position with good drainage.

Darwinia nieldiana

^^^

Fringed bell
Myrtaceae
WA

An attractive small shrub found on sandplains from Perth, north to Dongara. It is a multi-branched shrub to 60 cm high with crowded, linear, pointed leaves about 1 cm long. The reddish, pendant flower heads to around 5 cm across are surrounded by a number of fringed bracts. They appear from late winter through to December. This species needs an open position in a light, well-drained soil.

Darwinia oldfieldii

^^^

MYRTACEAE

WA

An attractive multi-branched shrub to 1 m found in sandplains in the Murchison River area. It has small, oblong, grey-green leaves edged with a light fringe of hairs. The flower heads are composed of up to twelve deep red flowers with long protruding styles. They are produced in late winter and early spring. In cultivation it prefers lots of sun, good drainage and a layer of mulch to protect the root system.

Darwinia purpurea

^^^

ROSE DARWINIA

MYRTACEAE

WA

This small, spreading shrub grows on sandy soils and near granite outcrops inland from Perth to around Merredin and north to Mullewa. It grows to only around 70 cm high with a spread of 1 m. Tiny, grey-green, oblong leaves are crowded along the branches. The terminal, dark crimson flowers with protruding styles are surrounded by short bracts. Flowers are produced in profusion during spring.

Daviesia pachyphylla

^^^

OUCH BUSH

FABACEAE

WA

This showy species is common on open heaths between Ongerup and Ravensthorpe. It has spreading, open branches to 1.5 m in height and has thick, succulent, terete leaves which taper to a sharp point. Abundant orange and dark red pea flowers are borne in loose clusters in the upper axils in late winter and early spring. This species is not well known in cultivation.

Diplolaena angustifolia

^^^

NATIVE ROSE, YANCHEP ROSE

RUTACEAE

WA

A graceful shrub to 1 m high found not far from the coast of Perth, north to Dongara. It has velvety branches and narrow, linear leaves to 5 cm long with rolled under margins and a whitish, felted undersurface. The prominent red or orange stamens are grouped in dense, pendant flower heads, surrounded by rows of bracts. These are produced from late winter to mid spring.

Dodonaea lobulata

^^^

LOBED-LEAF HOP-BUSH

SAPINDACEAE

WA, SA, NSW

Widespread in semi-arid parts and a conspicuous plant of the Kalgoorlie area, this ornamental shrub is noted for its colourful, reddish, three-winged capsules. The flowers are insignificant. It has shiny leaves with small, rounded lobes. They may be up to 5 cm in length and are sometimes rather sticky to the touch. This decorative species can be obtained from native plant nurseries. It is ideally suited to dry country gardens in a sunny, well-drained position.

Dodonaea microzyga

^^^

BRILLIANT HOP-BUSH

SAPINDACEAE

WA, SA, NT, QLD, NSW

This upright sticky shrub to 1.5 m high has a wide distribution and can be found in many regions of Central Australia. The small leaves, less than 1.5 cm long, are composed of three to seven tiny leaflets notched at the tip. The inconspicuous flowers are followed by prolific, bright red, three- to four-winged capsules. This species is seldom cultivated, but would make an attractive plant for low rainfall areas.

Drosera glanduligera

^^^

SCARLET SUNDEW, PIMPERNEL SUNDEW
DROSERACEAE
WA, SA, NSW, VIC, TAS

A delightful small, insectivorous plant found along wet banks and in moist soils. It is common in southern Australia. The yellowish-green leaves form a neat rosette up to 3 cm across. The erect flower stem to 10 cm tall bears up to twenty bright orange flowers with blackish centres, mostly during spring. There are over fifty species of sundews found in Australia. They trap insects on specialised tentacle-like hairs found mostly on the upper surface of the leaf. When an insect touches the tentacle it is entangled within seconds. The trapped insect is digested by means of a secretion released by glandular hairs.

Dryandra formosa

^^^

SHOWY DRYANDRA
PROTEACEAE
WA

This tall shrub with open branches reaches about 5 m in height. In exposed situations such as the seafront around Albany or the windswept slopes of the Stirling Range it can sometimes be seen as a stunted shrub. It has long narrow leaves which are deeply divided to the mid-rib and beautiful, large, deep-orange flowers with a metallic sheen. This dryandra is popular in cultivation and will grow on a variety of soils provided drainage is good.

Dryandra nivea

^^^

Couch honeypot
Proteaceae
WA

A widespread prostrate or low growing species that rarely exceeds 1 m in height. Its native habitat is on sandy and gravelly soils and it is common in the south-west of Western Australia. The decorative, finely divided leaves are dark green with a white, felted undersurface. The orange-brown flower heads in late winter and spring are set among the leaves and held very close to the ground. This interesting dryandra is sometimes seen in cultivation where, like most other dryandras, it demands good drainage.

Dryandra speciosa

^^^

Shaggy dryandra
Proteaceae
WA

This species is easy to identify as its entire leaves, unlike those of most dryandras, are not toothed. It is a small, erect shrub of a little more than 1 m in height. The pendulous flowers have brownish-grey outer bracts covering the orangey-pink flowers within. Flowers appear mostly in late winter and spring. Once established it is quite hardy in cultivation providing drainage is good.

Eremaea beaufortioides

^^^

ROUND-LEAVED EREMAEA
MYRTACEAE
WA

A small, many-branched shrub to 1.5 m high. It has spreading, recurved, ovate leaves to 6 mm long and terminal flowers composed of bundles of vivid orange flowers. Flowers are often abundant and in spring plants are conspicuous on the sandheaths north of Perth. This beautiful native plant has been cultivated by enthusiasts for many years and is available from some specialist nurseries. It prefers full sun and a lightly textured soil with excellent drainage. It resents humidity.

Eremophila decipiens

^^^

SLENDER FUCHSIA
MYOPORACEAE
WA, SA

This branched, sticky shrub extends from the Murchison River in Western Australia, across the Nullarbor Plain and into South Australia. It grows to around 2 m tall with linear to lanceolate leaves with a pointed tip. The bright red or orange tubular flowers have four upper lobes and one curled-back lower lobe. Flowers are held on slender S-shaped pedicles. Flowers can be seen from late winter to early summer.

Eremophila glabra

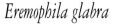

^^^

COMMON EMU-BUSH
MYOPORACEAE
WA, NT, SA, QLD, NSW, VIC

This very variable plant is seen throughout the drier areas of Australia in many forms and flower colours. It ranges in height from prostrate to around 1.5 m. The linear-lanceolate leaves are very variable, sometimes smooth or densely hairy and with or without serrations on the margins. Often young growth and leaves are sticky to the touch. The tubular flowers can be yellow, green, orange or red and appear mostly in spring and summer. The Murchison River form photographed has silver, velvety leaves and contrasting large, red flowers.

Eremophila maculata

^^^

NATIVE FUCHSIA
MYOPORACEAE
WA, NT, SA, QLD, NSW, VIC

This widely grown native plant also has a wide natural distribution and is found in many of the drier parts of the continent. It varies in height from 50 cm to 3 m tall and has slightly pointed, linear to lanceolate leaves to 5 cm long. The tubular flowers come in a variety of colours and shades of white, pink, yellow, red and purple, often with spotted throats. They are carried on S-shaped pedicles. Flowers have four pointed upper lobes and one curled-back lower lobe which is deeply cut below the middle of the corolla. Flowering time is mostly in winter and spring. It will grow in well-drained soils.

Eremophila racemosa

^^^

MYOPORACEAE

WA

This wonderful multi-coloured plant is difficult to place in a book of this type. The flowers begin life yellow, then change to orange, pink, magenta and deepen to red with age. Flowering time is mostly during spring. It comes from around north of Ravensthorpe and is a colourful beauty in the garden. It is a small erect shrub to no more than 2 m high with light green, narrow leaves broadening towards the tip. In the garden it prefers a sunny, well-drained position.

Eucalyptus caesia

^^^

GUNGURRU

MYRTACEAE

WA

This beautiful weeping mallee or small tree is often seen in cultivation but is rare in the wild and occurs naturally only around the base of a few isolated granite slopes in the central wheatbelt regions of southern Western Australia. It has deciduous, longitudinal curled bark. Upper stems, buds and fruits have a whitish, frosted appearance. The grey-green, lanceolate leaves are up to 20 cm long. Pendant red or pink flowers with yellow anthers hang in threes, followed by urn-shaped fruits to 3 cm long. Flowers are produced in winter or early spring. It does best in areas of low humidity.

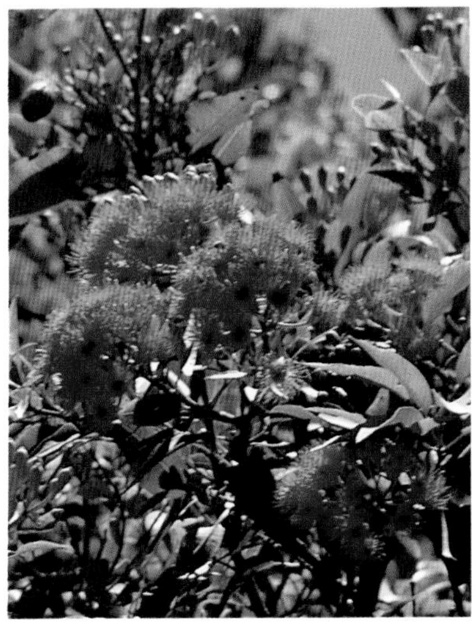

Eucalyptus ficifolia

^^^

RED-FLOWERING GUM
MYRTACEAE
WA

This very famous flowering gum occurs naturally only in a very restricted area from around Denmark to Walpole in the south-west of Western Australia. It is a small tree to 9 m high with rough, persistent bark and deep green, lanceolate leaves. In mid summer the clusters of pear-shaped buds open to a spectacular display of bright red, crimson, pink and sometimes cream flowers to 4 cm across. These are followed by large urn-shaped fruits. In cultivation it prefers a light, well-drained soil in a frost-free location.

Eucalyptus forrestiana

^^^

FUCHSIA MALLEE
MYRTACEAE
WA

This very attractive small tree or mallee to around 6 m high has found favour in roadside plantings particularly in semi-arid areas. It occurs naturally in a restricted area between Salmon Gums and Gibson north of Esperance and can easily be spotted from the car on the road to Norseman. Young branches are quadrangular and often red. It has thick, deep green, lanceolate leaves and drooping, bright red, four-sided flower buds to 5 cm long. These open to reveal short, bright yellow stamens. Flowers appear in spring, summer and autumn followed by winged four-sided fruits.

Eucalyptus macrocarpa

MOTTLECAH
MYRTACEAE
WA

This untidy, sprawling mallee grows on sandheaths from just north of Geraldton southwards to around Corrigin. Young angular branches, foliage and buds are powdery-grey. It has opposite, sessile, ovate leaves and large solitary flowers with red or pink filaments and yellow anthers. Flowers can be seen during the spring months. The large hemispherical fruits with prominent valves up to 9 cm in diameter are the largest among the eucalypts. This species does best in semi-arid areas with excellent drainage and a lightly textured soil.

Eucalyptus tetraptera

FOUR-WINGED MALLEE
MYRTACEAE
WA

This wonderful sprawling mallee can be seen in southern sandy heathlands from the Stirling Range east to around Israelite Bay. It has thick, leathery, broad-lanceolate leaves with a prominent mid-rib. The bright scarlet flower buds on a short, twisted peduncle, occur singly and open to reveal pinky-red filaments. Flowers occur mainly during the spring months. At first the quadrangular fruit to around 5 cm long is scarlet but turns brown and woody with age. It will grow in a protected coastal garden and does best in fairly dry areas.

Eucalyptus torquata

^^^

CORAL GUM
MYRTACEAE
WA

This beautiful small tree to around 11 m tall can be seen growing naturally in red, stony soil along the roadside from Norseman to Kalgoorlie. It also grows successfully as an ornamental street and park tree in Kalgoorlie and Alice Springs. It has grey-green, lanceolate leaves often with hooked tips. Clusters of up to seven, red, ribbed buds, with a narrow, horn-like extension, open to release paler red or pink filaments. These appear in spring and summer. This species is resistant to drought and is therefore ideal for dry country gardens.

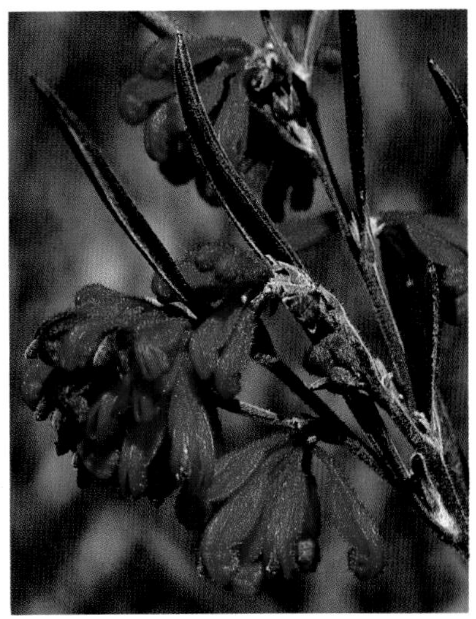

Grevillea brachystylis

^^^

PROTEACEAE
WA

This outstanding grevillea bears masses of velvety, red flowers with blue tipped styles. It occurs naturally in moist areas of the south-west of Western Australia and can be seen in forested areas around Busselton. It varies in habit and may be upright to 2 m high or a sprawling small shrub to 60 cm high. The narrow leaves to 14 cm have recurved margins and may be covered in hairs, especially when young. This beautiful shrub is fairly new to cultivation. It needs a well-drained position, but must be kept moist during hot dry weather. Tip prune regularly to encourage bushy habit.

Grevillea dielsiana

^^^

PROTEACEAE
WA

This multi-branched shrub to around 2 m high occurs on the Murchison River sandplains. It has prickly foliage divided into a further three terete leaflets. The pendant, red, orange or pinky-yellow flowers in rather loose racemes are very numerous during winter and spring. In cultivation this species requires a warm situation with excellent drainage and full sun. Tip prune regularly to prevent it from becoming straggly.

Grevillea insignis

^^^

PROTEACEAE
WA

Another beautiful grevillea found on the southern sandplains and heath of Western Australia. It is an erect shrub to 4 m with wavy, holly-like leaves with prickly lobes. The clusters of reddish-pink flowers are abundantly produced during winter and spring. This species is best suited to a warm climate away from high humidity.

Grevillea juncifolia

^^^

HONEYSUCKLE GREVILLEA
PROTEACEAE
WA, SA, NT, QLD, NSW

This tall erect shrub to 4 m is conspicuous in arid regions of Australia. Its showy, bright orange, cylindrical flowers up to 15 cm long are borne at the ends of branches. They are rich in nectar making this a popular honey plant of the Aborigines. This is an attractive species for dry inland gardens. Prune regularly to encourage compact growth.

Grevillea nudiflora

^^^

PROTEACEAE
WA

A small, spreading or prostrate shrub of the southern sandplains of Western Australia. It has trailing or arching branches and light green, linear leaves up to 25 cm long. Small clusters of bright red flowers are produced on leafless branches in late winter and spring. This species has adapted well to cultivation and is especially suited to rockeries and banks where the trailing branches can be displayed to advantage.

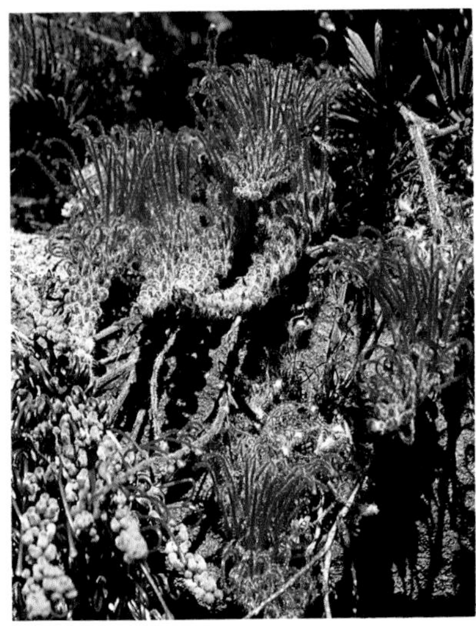

Grevillea thyrsoides

^^^

Proteaceae

WA

This wonderful plant occurs on dry sandy soils of the northern wheatbelt region of Western Australia. It is a low-spreading shrub covered in short, woolly hairs. The grey-green, pinnate leaves are composed of up to fourteen pairs of leaflets. Toothbrush-shaped flowers are a deep reddish-pink and are extremely hairy. They have a very long flowering period through winter to mid summer. This is a very attractive rockery plant for well-drained, open positions in full sun.

Grevillea tripartita

^^^

Proteaceae

WA

An attractive upright shrub to over 2 m tall found on sandheaths in the Fitzgerald River National Park. The prickly, grey-green leaves are divided into three to five leaflets. Showy clusters of red and yellow flowers with a protruding style appear in spring and summer. In cultivation this grevillea is best suited to an open, dry position with good drainage.

Grevillea wilsonii

^^^

WILSON'S GREVILLEA
PROTEACEAE
WA

This multi-branched, spreading shrub to 1 m is common in the jarrah forests of the south-west of Western Australia. It is an outstanding plant of the bush, having vivid scarlet flowers atop finely divided, sharp-pointed leaves. This popular shrub in cultivation does best in a fairly dry location in a well-drained soil and a sunny position.

Hakea francisiana

^^^

NARUKALIA
PROTEACEAE
WA, SA

A lovely large shrub or small tree up to 5 m or more high. It grows on sandy plains and shrublands of Western Australia and South Australia. The greyish-green leaves to 26 cm long are prominently marked with longitudinal veins. Attractive deep pink or red flowers in elongated spikes to 10 cm long are borne from the leaf axils from mid winter to late spring. This very decorative species is best suited to semi-arid gardens. It must have good drainage and a sunny position.

Hakea laurina

^^^

PINCUSHION HAKEA
PROTEACEAE
WA

This old favourite of cultivation occurs naturally on the southern sandplains of Western Australia. It is a large shrub to 8 m high with flat, broadly-linear leaves up to 15 cm long with conspicuous longitudinal veins. The red flowers packed into rounded balls are covered with thin, cream-coloured stamens. They are produced in the upper axils in autumn and winter. This most attractive hakea has proved adaptable to many soil types and situations. Protect from strong winds and lightly prune from early days to maintain shape.

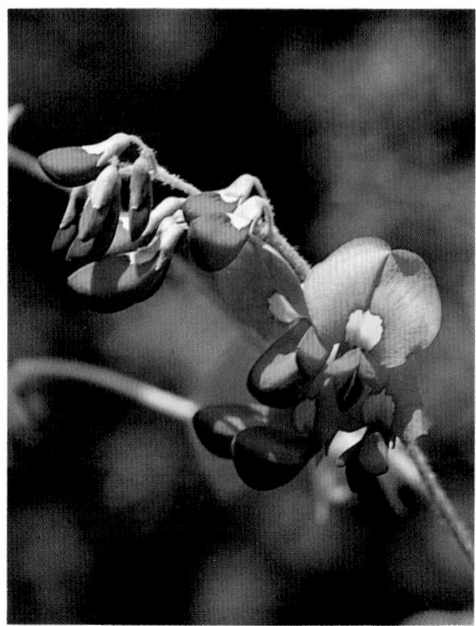

Kennedia macrophylla

^^^

FABACEAE
WA

This vigorous climbing plant is regarded as endangered in its natural habitat and is confined to coastal dunes in the Augusta district. It has long, twisted, trailing stems and light green leaves divided into three obovate leaflets up to 6 cm long. Young leaves are covered in silky hairs. The dull red, pea flowers are carried in racemes up to 15 cm long in late spring and summer. This species is well known in cultivation and is usually available from nurseries specialising in native plants. It grows in most well-drained soils, but requires protection from heavy frost.

Kennedia prostrata

^^^

RUNNING POSTMAN
FABACEAE
ALL STATES

This very pretty creeping plant is common in coastal areas but is also found inland on creek banks. It has a neat spread of up to 2 m. It has small, wavy leaflets in threes and produces numerous, bright red, pea flowers in late winter and spring. In the garden it makes an attractive groundcover and rockery plant and can be grown in full or partial sun.

Kunzea pulchella

^^^

GRANITE KUNZEA
MYRTACEAE
WA

This most attractive shrub grows in the crevices of granite rocks in the drier areas of the south-west of Western Australia. It is an irregularly shaped shrub to 3 m and has grey-green, ovate leaves covered in silky hairs. The bright red flowers are produced in short, dense clusters mostly during winter and spring. This is an ornamental bird-attracting plant for the garden where it is best suited to semi-arid districts.

Lambertia inermis

^^^

CHITTICK
PROTEACEAE
WA

A common plant of deep sands in southern Western Australia especially from Albany to Israelite Bay. It grows from 2 to 4 m high and has flat, obovate to linear leaves to 2 cm long. The clusters of orange flowers are in heads of seven. These are produced mostly during spring and summer, but blooms can be found throughout the year.

Lambertia multiflora

^^^

MANY-FLOWERED HONEYSUCKLE
PROTEACEAE
WA

This many-branched shrub to around 1.5 m tall is common on sandy heaths north of Perth. The flat, linear leaves with revolute margins end with a pointed tip. The terminal, red or yellow flowers in clusters of seven are produced throughout the year.

Lechenaultia formosa

^^^

RED LECHENAULTIA
GOODENIACEAE
WA

This small, spreading plant to around 30 cm high is widespread in the south-west of Western Australia. It has crowded, fleshy terete leaves to 1 cm long and bears pink to bright red flowers in late winter and spring. This species has been cultivated for many years and there are many colour forms available. It is best suited to a well-drained, sandy soil in an open sunny position. It is also an excellent choice for pots and hanging baskets.

Leucopogon verticillatus

^^^

TASSEL FLOWER
EPACRIDACEAE
WA

This is a common understorey shrub of the karri and jarrah forests of the south-west of Western Australia. It grows up to 3 m or more high and has whorled lanceolate leaves up to 15 cm in length. Small reddish flowers borne in slender sprays arise from the leaf axils during spring. This species is uncommon in cultivation.

Lysiana exocarpi

^^^

HARLEQUIN MISTLETOE
LORANTHACEAE
WA, SA, NT, QLD, NSW, VIC

This parasitic plant found in central Australia occurs on a wide range of hosts including *Allocasuarina*, *Acacia*, *Eremophila* and *Cassia* species. It has flat, linear to oblong leaves to 15 cm long and red, tubular flowers borne in the leaf axils. They are usually produced in twos or threes on a short common stalk. The red or black fruit is ovoid, succulent and up to 1 cm long.

Maireana sedifolia

^^^

BLUEBUSH
CHENOPODIACEAE
WA, SA, NSW, VIC

This small, branched shrub to 1 m is a common bluebush of the Nullarbor Plain. It has bluish-grey, small, succulent leaves to 1 cm. The flowers are inconspicuous but develop into very attractive, bright, reddish-pink, flattish fruit to 1 cm across with wavy edges.

Melaleuca elliptica

^^^

GRANITE BOTTLEBRUSH
MYRTACEAE
WA

This branched shrub to 4 m high occurs amongst granite outcrops in southern coastal areas of Western Australia and inland to the Coolgardie district. It has opposite, ovate leaves to 1.5 cm long. The showy, dark red flowers are borne in dense, oblong spikes, up to 6 cm long on the older branches in spring and summer. An attractive garden shrub for a sunny, well-drained position.

Melaleuca fulgens

^^^

SCARLET HONEY MYRTLE
MYRTACEAE
WA

A popular garden shrub that occurs naturally in the dry wheatbelt regions of Western Australia. It is a slender, open shrub to 2 m high with opposite linear leaves to 2.5 cm long. The showy, red flowers are displayed in rather loose, oblong spikes, the axis of which continues to grow after flowering. Flowers appear during spring. This attractive species is available from many nurseries and suits a sunny, open, well-drained position in the garden. It will withstand dry periods.

Melaleuca lateritia

^^^

ROBIN REDBREAST BUSH
MYRTACEAE
WA

This multi-branched shrub to 2 m occurs in swamps in the coastal areas of south-west Western Australia. It has alternate, pointed, linear leaves to 2 cm long. The large, orange-red flowers are arranged in oblong brushes to 5 cm long. Flowers are produced on old wood and appear in spring and summer and sometimes again in autumn. This decorative, bird-attracting species likes a moist, but well-drained position in cultivation.

Nematolepis phebalioides

^^^

RUTACEAE
WA

This is the only species in this genus. It is confined to the south coastal area between Israelite Bay and Lake Grace and occurs naturally in heaths and mallee country. It is an attractive upright shrub to 1 m and has neat, oval, glossy leaves with a scaly undersurface. Pendulous, bright red, tubular flowers tipped with green and protruding yellow stamens are produced in spring.

Oxylobium parviflorum

^^^

BOX POISON
FABACEAE
WA

This colourful understorey shrub is widespread in south-west Western Australia and a number of forms exist. The common form is an erect shrub to 1.2 m high with dark green, oval to oblong leaves with a silky undersurface. The orange and red flowers are borne in racemes mainly at branch ends during spring. This species is known to be extremely poisonous to stock.

Prostanthera magnifica

^^^

MAGNIFICENT MINT BUSH
LAMIACEAE
WA

This extremely attractive plant occurs in sandy areas around Geraldton and further inland to Payne's Find. It is a spreading shrub up to 2 m high with thick, lanceolate leaves up to 2.5 cm long. The flowers vary in colour from pale lilac or pink, but it is the much enlarged deep red, magenta or purple calyx that makes this plant so noticeable. Flowering time is from late winter to early summer. In cultivation this plant resents humidity and must have excellent drainage in a light, sandy soil.

Santalum acuminatum

^^^

Quandong
Santalaceae
WA, NT, SA, Qld, NSW

This shrub or small tree up to 6 m high is found in numerous woodland communities throughout drier inland areas though never in great numbers. It has a slight pendulous habit with pale, yellowish-green, lanceolate leaves to 7 cm long which taper to a curved point. The tiny cream flowers are followed by rounded fruit to 3 cm in diameter maturing to bright red. When ripe the flesh is edible, either raw or when used in jams or preserves. The round, pitted nuts have been used to make necklaces, Chinese checkers and marbles.

Stirlingia latifolia

^^^

Blueboy, Broad-leaf stirlingia
Proteaceae
WA

This small shrub to 1.5 m high occurs in the Stirling Range, from where the genus gets its name. It is also found in sandheaths from Busselton to Three Springs. It has grey-green leaves to 30 cm long divided into flat lobes. The orange-red flowers are borne in dense round heads on branched panicles. These are produced during spring.

Templetonia retusa

^^^

COCKIES' TONGUES, PARROT BUSH

FABACEAE

WA, SA

This is the most attractive and best known species of *Templetonia*. It is often seen when travelling in coastal areas of the south-west from Geraldton to the Great Australian Bight. It is a spreading shrub to 1.5 m high with grey-green entire leaves and large, deep pink, scarlet or dull red, pea flowers up to 6 cm long. These are produced from late winter to mid spring. There is also a cream flower form.

Verticordia grandis

^^^

SCARLET FEATHER FLOWER

MYRTACEAE

WA

This is one of the most spectacular of the feather flowers and can be seen in the coastal sandplains north of Perth. It is a straggling, spreading shrub from 1 to 2 m tall and across. Neat, stem-clasping, rounded leaves are set in pairs along the stems. The large scarlet flowers are thickly fringed and have long projecting styles. They are produced from the upper leaf axils and form brilliant spikes up to 12 cm long during the spring months.

^^^ *Purple and Blue* ^^^

F·L·O·W·E·R·S

Alyogyne huegelii

^^^

LILAC HIBISCUS

MALVACEAE

WA, SA

An attractive somewhat resinous shrub that is widely distributed in the south-west of Western Australia to the Lofty Ranges in South Australia. It grows up to 2.5 m high and has deeply lobed leaves to 7 cm long. The white, mauve or purple, hibiscus-like flowers are produced in spring and summer. This popular native plant in cultivation will adapt to a wide range of soil types in a sunny or partly shaded position. Prune after flowering to prevent straggly growth.

Brachyscome iberidifolia

^^^

SWAN RIVER DAISY

ASTERACEAE

WA, NT, SA

This very pretty annual is widespread and can be found growing along watercourses, on sandhills and plains and among granite outcrops. It is a slender plant to 50 cm high with light green, finely divided leaves to 3 cm long. Small, daisy-like flowers in white and shades of blue and purple are produced mostly in spring and summer. Packets of seeds are readily available. Sow seeds directly where they are to grow during winter in frost-free districts.

Calectasia cyanea

^^^

BLUE TINSEL LILY
CALECTASIACEAE
WA

This beautiful wildflower lights up the bush with its wonderful iridescent colours. It is widespread in the south-west of Western Australia and can be found in heath and low, open woodland. The plant has a suckering habit and grows only to about 50 cm high. It has narrow, linear leaves to 1.5 cm long and deep blue or purple, star-like flowers with yellow anthers which turn orange or red with age. These appear mostly from winter to mid spring.

Chamaescilla corymbosa

^^^

BLUE STARS, BLUE SQUILL
LILIACEAE
WA, SA, NSW, VIC

This pretty little perennial has a wide distribution over southern Australia where it is usually found in moist sites in grasslands and woodlands. It only reaches up to around 15 cm high and has grass-like leaves arising from a tuberous rootstock. The six-petalled, blue or purple flowers are carried in loose clusters at the ends of slender stems during spring.

Cyanostegia corifolia

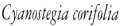

^^^

Dicrastylidaceae
WA

This highly attractive shrub of the drier parts of south-west Western Australia can be seen growing along roadsides in sandy or gravelly soil. It is a rather resinous shrub to 1.5 m tall with leathery, wedge-shaped leaves up to 4 cm long. The flowers are a deep purple-blue and are surrounded by a conspicuous papery calyx of a paler colour. They are produced in profusion in long panicles and make a spectacular showing from late winter to early summer.

Dampiera diversifolia

^^^

Goodeniaceae
WA

A colourful, mat forming plant with a spread of up to 2 m across. The toothed leaves at the base of the plant are narrow and lanceolate while those further up the stem widen towards the tip. Numerous vivid purple-blue flowers are produced along the stems from late winter through to summer. This beautiful suckering plant is excellent for use as a groundcover, rockery and hanging basket specimen. It is available from many nurseries that sell native plants.

Dampiera eriocephala

^^^

WOOLLY-HEADED DAMPIERA
GOODENIACEAE
WA

This species is found in sandy soils in fairly dry areas of south-west Western Australia. It is often more prolific after fire in burnt areas. It is a perennial with dark green, oval leaves which widen towards the tip and have a conspicuous woolly-white undersurface. The deep blue flowers are borne in dense terminal heads on leafless woolly stems. Flowers during spring.

Dampiera linearis

^^^

COMMON DAMPIERA
GOODENIACEAE
WA

This widespread and variable species is found in many habitats in southern Western Australia. It is a perennial herb which spreads by suckering and grows to around 50 cm tall. The leaves are sometimes toothed and can be linear to cuneate from 1 to 4 cm long. The purple or blue flowers are covered with grey hairs on the outside. Flowers appear during winter and spring.

Dampiera trigona

^^^

ANGLED-STEM DAMPIERA
GOODENIACEAE
WA

This wispy perennial herb occurs in areas near the coast north and south of Perth. It has very slender, three-angled stems to around 50 cm high and scattered linear to lanceolate leaves to 4 cm long sometimes with a few teeth. Dainty purple or blue flowers are borne on slim stems from late winter through to mid summer.

Elythranthera brunonis

^^^

PURPLE ENAMEL ORCHID
ORCHIDACEAE
WA

This delightful, tiny, terrestrial orchid has a wide distribution in south-west Western Australia from Esperance in the south to just north of Perth. It can also be seen growing in Kings Park. It grows only to 30 cm high when in flower, has one dark green, lance-shaped leaf to 8 cm and bears dark purple, glossy flowers, up to three per stem, from late winter to early summer.

Eremophila christopheri

^^^

MYOPORACEAE
NT

This beautiful plant of the desert grows along creeks and at the base of stony hillsides in the Macdonnell Ranges. It grows to around 2 m high and has bright green, crowded, narrow to lanceolate leaves which end in a pointed tip. The blue or lavender tubular flowers to 2 cm long, lightly hairy on the outside, have pointed lobes. Flowers appear mostly during winter, but can be seen at other times.

Eremophila densifolia

^^^

MYOPORACEAE
WA

This small, spreading plant usually occurs in red soils in semi-arid regions of southern Western Australia. It grows to no more than 50 cm high and has crowded, very narrow-linear or terete leaves which are quite hairy and can be tinged with purple. The blue or purple tubular flowers with spreading pointed lobes, are carried near the ends of the branches from late winter to early summer.

Eremophila drummondii

^^^

MYOPORACEAE
WA

This showy wildflower occurs in sandy heaths and woodlands in the drier parts of southern Western Australia. It grows to around 2 m high with lots of slender branches and narrow-linear leaves to 5 cm long. New growth and leaves are sticky to the touch. Masses of blue or violet tubular flowers are borne singly or in pairs along the branches from late winter and during spring.

Eremophila gilesii

^^^

DESERT FUCHSIA
MYOPORACEAE
WA, NT, SA, QLD, NSW

A small sticky shrub found in mulga country throughout the arid regions of Central Australia. It grows to around 1 m high, is sparsely pubescent and has felted, slender, grey-green leaves to 6 cm long with a channel above, ending with a pointed tip. The pink, lilac or purple pendulous flowers, hairy on the outside, have large spreading lobes. The stamens are enclosed. Flowers appear chiefly in winter and spring.

Eremophila goodwinii

^^^

PURPLE FUCHSIA-BUSH
MYOPORACEAE
NT, QLD, NSW

This slender sticky shrub inhabits red or sandy soils and dry stony sand of Central Australia. It grows to around 1.5 m high and is lightly coated with hairs. The narrow-linear, grey-green leaves to 7 cm long are hairy and sticky and end with a curved point. The tubular, pale purple flowers, lightly hairy on the outside, have pointed lobes and almost hidden stamens. Flowers appear in winter and spring.

Eremophila macdonnellii

^^^

MYOPORACEAE
NT, SA, QLD, NSW

This small variable shrub from the dry interior may be prostrate or upright to around 1 m high. It also varies in density of hair covering on branches and leaves. The stem-clasping leaves may be linear, oblong to ovate and depending on locations may have a whitish bloom. The slightly flattened, tubular flowers to around 3.5 cm long have rounded flower lobes. Flowers in spring and summer.

Eremophila merrallii

^^^

MYOPORACEAE

WA

A showy dwarf species from the Southern Cross area in Western Australia where it occurs as an understorey shrub to eucalypts. It reaches only 50 cm high. Branches, leaves and parts of the flower are coated with hairs. The almost terete, crowded, grey-green leaves end with a blunt tip. Small mauve or lilac tubular flowers contrast beautifully with the grey-green leaves. Flowers are produced in the upper axils during spring and summer.

Glycine clandestina

^^^

TWINING GLYCINE

FABACEAE

WA, SA, QLD, NSW, VIC, TAS

This slender, twining, perennial plant occurs over a very wide area in a variety of habitats and is quite common in arid regions. The leaves consist of three linear leaflets to 4 cm long. The small pea flowers in shades of purple are borne in loose racemes in the upper axils. Flowering is mostly during spring and summer.

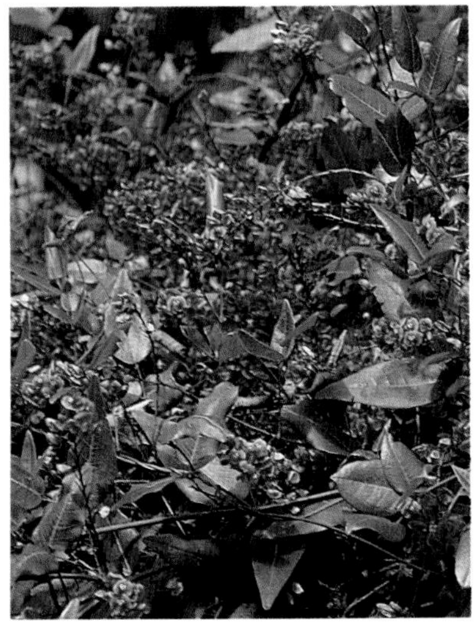

Hardenbergia comptoniana

^^^

NATIVE WISTERIA, WILD SARSAPARILLA
FABACEAE
WA

This beautiful creeper is common in the karri and jarrah forests as well as on the Swan Coastal Plain. It will climb or spread for up to 4 m and has dark green trifoliate leaves. Sprays of purple pea flowers are borne in profusion during spring. This species is widely cultivated and will grow in most soils with good drainage. It is suitable for a trellis and may be trained to cover fences or pergolas.

Hovea chorizemifolia

^^^

HOLLY-LEAVED HOVEA
FABACEAE
WA

This erect shrub to around 1 m or more high occurs in gravelly soils of the Darling Range and is easy to recognise by its prickly, holly-like leaves. In late winter and early spring it bears conspicuous purple, pea-shaped flowers in clusters along the top part of the branches. This species is uncommon in cultivation, but can be found at some specialist native plant nurseries.

Hovea elliptica

^^^

TREE HOVEA

FABACEAE

WA

When in flower this is a very noticeable understorey shrub of the karri and jarrah forests of the south-west of Western Australia. It may reach up to 4 m high and has dark green, lanceolate leaves. In the garden this species likes the protection of other plants and can be grown beneath trees. It needs good drainage.

Hovea pungens

^^^

DEVIL'S PINS

FABACEAE

WA

This species has a wide distribution over the south-west of Western Australia and is quite common around Perth. It is an erect shrub to around 1 m or more high and has prickly, narrow, dark green leaves to 2.5 cm long. It is extremely attractive in flower when masses of purple, pea flowers are borne along the upper branchlets in late winter and spring.

Hovea trisperma

^^^

COMMON HOVEA
FABACEAE
WA

This widespread and best known hovea is found on sandy soils in a variety of habitats in the south-west of Western Australia. It is a small shrub to 50 cm high with linear to lanceolate leaves to 5 cm long. Masses of small, purple, pea flowers are produced in small clusters towards branch ends mostly during the winter months. This is an attractive winter flowering plant for a container or rockery where it prefers a partly shaded, protected position and excellent drainage.

Keraudrenia hermanniaefolia

^^^

CRINKLE-LEAVED FIREBUSH
STERCULIACEAE
WA

This small, spreading shrub to less than 1 m high is found in the sandy tracts and heaths from Wongan Hills northwards to Shark Bay. It has dark green, wavy-edged, crinkly leaves to around 1 cm in length. The showy flowers are produced in loose clusters at branch ends during spring. The showy part of the flower is the enlarged, five-lobed calyx which is coloured purple.

Lechenaultia biloba

^^^

Blue lechenaultia
Goodeniaceae
WA

This beautiful, blue wildflower occurs naturally in gravelly and sandy soils in a variety of habitats from Three Springs south to Cape Leewin and inland to Lake King. It forms an open spreading plant to 50 cm high with soft terete leaves to 1 cm long. The open flowers up to 3 cm across come in various shades of blue and almost cover the plant when in full flower. Flowering is usually from late winter to late spring. In the garden it is essential that it is grown in a light, well-drained soil.

Lechenaultia floribunda

^^^

Free-flowering lechenaultia
Goodeniaceae
WA

This pretty, small shrub to less than 1 m high is found in the sandy tracts of the coastal plain from Perth northwards to Shark Bay. It has crowded, soft terete leaves to 7 mm long and bears numerous, small, terminal flowers from late winter to early summer. The colour varies from almost white to pale blue or pale mauve. This species is uncommon in cultivation.

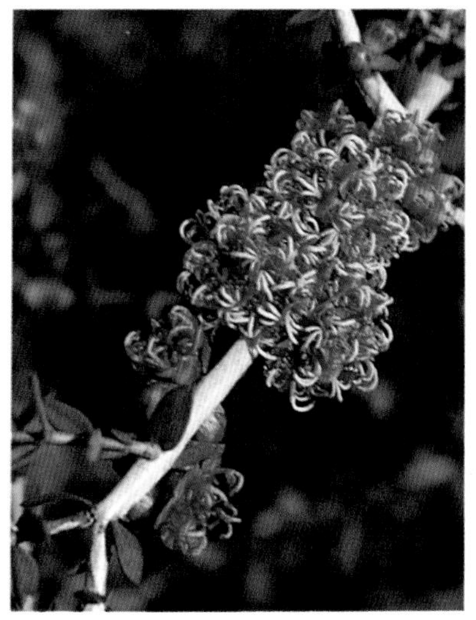

Melaleuca violacea

^^^

VIOLET HONEY MYRTLE
MYRTACEAE
WA

A small shrub to 1.5 m high that occurs mostly in coastal areas of southern Western Australia. It has small, stem-clasping, ovate leaves and clusters of small violet to purple flowers. This is a very pretty, small garden plant suited to a moist sunny position. Prune after flowering to encourage compact habit.

Orthrosanthus laxus

^^^

MORNING IRIS
IRIDACEAE
WA

This pretty, perennial herb to 55 cm tall has a wide distribution in south-west Western Australia from Geraldton to Albany. It has erect, grass-like leaves to 45 cm long and blue flowers in loose panicles in late winter and spring. The flowers open early in the morning and wither during the day.

Patersonia occidentalis

^^^

PURPLE FLAG

IRIDACEAE

WA, SA, VIC, TAS

This tussock forming herb has a wide distribution in temperate coastal regions and is common around Perth. The linear, flat, grass-like leaves to 55 cm long are finely veined. Abundant purple flowers open for one day only in spring through to early summer.

Scaevola striata

^^^

ROYAL ROBE

GOODENIACEAE

WA

This very pretty, low growing plant has a spread of up to 1 m across. It is common on gravelly soils of the Darling Range and jarrah forests as far north as Mogumber to the south coast. It has hairy stems and coarsely-toothed leaves to 5 cm long. The deep purple flowers to 3 cm across have striations on the petals. They are produced at branch ends during spring and summer. In the garden this small showy plant makes a good rockery subject.

Solanum ellipticum

^^^

POTATO BUSH, POTATO WEED
SOLANACEAE
WA, NT, SA, QLD, NSW

Widespread in Central Australia this spreading perennial herb grows on a variety of soils from stony and heavy clay to sandy. It has densely pubescent stems and grey-green, ovate to elliptic leaves to 8 cm long often with wavy margins. Prickles up to 1 cm long are on stems and calyx and may be present on other parts of the plant including the leaves. The purple flowers with triangular lobes are followed by edible greenish berries often tinged purple. The berries are an Aboriginal food source.

Solanum ferocissimum

^^^

SOLANACEAE
WA, NT, SA, QLD, NSW

This erect slender shrub to around 1 m occurs in drier parts of inland Australia, often in the shelter of other shrubs and trees. It has abundant slender prickles to 1 cm on stems, leaves and flower stalks and can be quite nasty if the unwary traveller gets caught in it. It has narrow, linear leaves to 4 cm and small, pale blue or purple flowers in groups of up to six. These are followed by small, shiny, red berries which age to almost black.

Solanum quadriloculatum

^^^

SOLANACEAE
WA, NT, SA, QLD

A robust, velvety-grey, low shrub to 50 cm common in arid regions of Central Australia. It has abundant prickles on stems, flower stalks and calyx. The large, felty, ovate leaves to 12 cm long are up to 6 cm broad. Purple flowers, in groups of up to twenty, are held above the leaves on stems up to 9 cm long. These are followed by yellowish-brown berries which become very hard with age.

Solanum sturtianum

^^^

THARGOMINDAH NIGHTSHADE
SOLANACEAE
WA, NT, SA, QLD, NSW

This erect, grey-green, slender shrub to 3 m tall is widespread across Central Australia. Prickles may be absent or there may be a few scattered on the stems. It has narrow, lanceolate leaves to 7 cm long often with wavy edges. The purple flowers are about 4 cm across when open. The globular berries are green or yellowish-brown at first and blacken when dry.

Sollya heterophylla

^^^

BLUEBELL CREEPER
PITTOSPORACEAE
WA

This shrub or semi-climber is common in forests and woodlands of the south-west of Western Australia. It has light, twining stems and oval, pointed leaves. The pendulous, bell-shaped, blue flowers are produced during spring and summer. These are followed by sprays of fleshy, blue fruits. This is an adaptable and popular species in cultivation and is readily available from general nurseries. It may be used to cover fences and trellises or allowed to cascade down banks.

Thysanotus patersonii

^^^

TWINING FRINGED LILY
LILIACEAE
ALL STATES

This interesting small plant has a very wide distribution and is quite common in the Darling Range, Western Australia. It begins life with a small clump of leaves at the base which it sheds as it grows, depending on its leafless, twining stems for photosynthesis. Numerous small, pale violet flowers with three-fringed petals are produced on short stems in early spring.

Thysanotus tuberosus

^^^

COMMON FRINGED LILY
LILIACEAE
ALL MAINLAND STATES

This is another widespread fringe lily. It is a very pretty, clump forming plant with a tuberous root system and erect, grass-like leaves. The flowering stems to 20 cm tall have loose panicles of purple flowers with three broad petals fringed at the edges. They are produced during the spring months.

Trichodesma zeylanicum

^^^

CATTLEBUSH
BORAGINACEAE
WA, NT, SA, QLD, NSW

This very widespread species is common in the centre as well as coastal and tropical areas. It is also found in Asia and Africa. It is an upright, perennial herb to 2 m tall often with rough, stiff hairs. It has lanceolate leaves up to 10 cm long and pale blue to deep blue nodding flowers throughout the winter months.

Green and unusually coloured

F·L·O·W·E·R·S

Anigozanthos viridis

^^^

GREEN KANGAROO PAW
HAEMODORACEAE
WA

This eye-catching species occurs in winter-wet clay soils on the west coast from Moora southwards to the Busselton district. It has long, flat or almost tube-like leaves to 30 cm long and metallic-green flowers on stems to 50 cm high in late winter and spring. The whole of this attractive plant is in various shades of green. It is often cultivated and is best suited to a moist, lightly-shaded situation.

Boronia clavata

^^^

RUTACEAE
WA

A bushy shrub to 2 m high with dark-green aromatic divided leaves composed of three to seven very narrow leaflets. The lime-green flowers, hanging bell-like along the stem, are lightly scented. They are produced in spring and early summer. This attractive and adaptable species is one of the easiest boronias to grow. It prefers good drainage and some shade.

Boronia megastigma

^^^

Brown boronia
Rutaceae
WA

This favourite wildflower of many people can be found growing naturally in and around swampy areas near Albany. It is a slender, open, aromatic shrub to 1.5 m high and has light green foliage composed of three narrow leaflets. The highly perfumed, rich brown and yellow bell flowers are produced in early spring. In cultivation this boronia needs a well-drained soil that is never allowed to dry out. A good mulch will keep the roots cool and moist. Prune back after flowering to prolong the life of the plant.

Cephalotus follicularis

^^^

Albany pitcher plant
Cephalotaceae
WA

This amazing little insectivorous plant grows in moist places and near the margins of swamps around the coastal district of Albany and near Busselton. It produces both normal, flat, oval leaves and modified leaves which assume the pitcher shape, topped with a small leaf which forms the lid. These collect and digest insects. When young they are bright green in colour and develop red and purple tonings as they mature. In late summer, an erect flower stalk bearing small white flowers is produced. This species is often cultivated by carnivorous-plant enthusiasts.

Eucalyptus lehmannii

^^^

Lehmann's mallee
Myrtaceae
WA

This fascinating plant is quite remarkable in bud, flower and fruit. It grows on sandy soils and can be seen from around Albany and the Stirling Range, eastward to Esperance and near Eucla. It is a mallee or small tree to 5 m high with deep green, lanceolate leaves tapering to a short point. The green or red flower buds (up to 20), around 5 cm long, are fused together at the base. As the buds open masses of yellow or light green filaments form large, rounded flower heads to about 12 cm across. These occur mostly in late winter and early spring followed by marvellous large, rounded woody fruits with pointed valves.

Hakea corymbosa

^^^

Cauliflower hakea
Proteaceae
WA

This compact, upright shrub occurs in deep sand from the Stirling Range to Esperance with an isolated population north of Perth. Very stiff, prickly-pointed leaves have a prominent central vein. The lime-green flowers are produced in terminal clusters at the top of the shrub in late winter and spring. In the garden grow in a light, well-drained soil in full sun.

Hakea victoria

^^^

ROYAL HAKEA
PROTEACEAE
WA

This most unusual plant grows mainly on heaths in the Fitzgerald River National Park with isolated populations on the lower hills of the Stirling Range. It is a tall, upright shrub to 3 m or more high with very large, serrated, cup-shaped leaves. The floral leaves are at first heavily marked with cream, but deepen to orange and then red as they age. There are also deep green juvenile leaves at the base of the plant. The white flowers are small and are deeply hidden in the leaves.

Kennedia nigricans

^^^

BLACK KENNEDIA, BLACK CORAL PEA
FABACEAE
WA

This outstanding climber is common on sandy soils in southern coastal areas from Cape Riche to Hopetoun. It has a vigorous spread and dark green, trifoliate leaves. The unusual black and yellow pea flowers to 3 cm long are borne in loose racemes during spring. This species is available from native plant nurseries. It is hardy and adaptable to a wide range of conditions, but is extremely rampant and will smother other garden subjects if planted too close.

Macropidia fuliginosa

^^^

BLACK KANGAROO PAW

HAEMODORACEAE

WA

A striking perennial plant found in sandy plains, heaths and woodlands north of Perth to Geraldton. It has flax-like leaves to 50 cm long and bears black and green flowers on branched, flowering stems up to 1 m tall or more. Both the stems and flowers are thickly covered with black hairs. This is an unusual species for growing in a container or a very well-drained, sandy soil. It needs plenty of sun and will not tolerate humid conditions.

Paraserianthes lophantha

^^^

CAPE WATTLE, SWAMP WATTLE

MIMOSACEAE

WA

This small tree occurs in swampy conditions in forested areas in south-west Western Australia. It grows up to 8 m tall and has soft, bipinnate foliage in up to twelve pairs. The scented, green, miniature, bottlebrush-like flowers occur from autumn through to spring. It is widely cultivated and is often sold under its old name *Albizia lophantha*. Being a fast grower it is useful for quick shade in a new garden or as a screening plant.

Pimelea physodes

^^^

QUALUP BELL
THYMELAEACEAE
WA

There is something rather exciting about finding this wonderful wildflower growing naturally on sandy heathlands and stony hills in the Fitzgerald River National Park and around Ravensthorpe. It grows to less than 1 m high with neat, oval, overlapping leaves. The clusters of small flowers are enclosed by large apple-green bracts which are tinged red and which deepen in colour as they age. These lovely bell-like flowers appear in late winter and spring. Unfortunately it is rarely seen in cultivation.

Pterostylis recurva

^^^

JUG ORCHID, JUG GREENHOOD
ORCHIDACEAE
WA, NT

This small terrestrial orchid is widespread in south-west Western Australia and is common in forested areas of the Darling Range. The specimen pictured was photographed in Kings Park, Perth. It grows to around 40 cm high and has delicate white flowers with prominent green or brown striations. Flowers can be seen in late winter and early spring.

Ptilotus macrocephalus

^^^

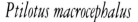

GREEN PUSSYTAIL
AMARANTHACEAE
ALL MAINLAND STATES

This beautiful widespread perennial of the inland is common in open sandplains and woodland communities. It grows to about 50 cm high with alternate, narrow, linear leaves to 5 cm long. The yellow-green flower heads in large oblong spikes to 12 cm long are borne at the ends of the stems in winter and spring.

Tersonia brevipes

^^^

BUTTON CREEPER
GYROSTEMONACEAE
WA

This unusual creeping plant looks as if it is made of plastic. It can be seen growing in coastal sandheaths from Kalbarri, south to Bunbury. It is a prostrate, perennial herb with greenish-yellow female flowers which develop into button-like fruit to 1.5 cm across.

Index of Botanical Names

Index of Common Names